Why I'm a Democrat

Why I'm a Democrat

Edited by
Susan Mulcahy

Foreword by David Brock

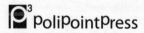 PoliPointPress

Why I'm a Democrat
Copyright © 2008 by Susan Mulcahy

An earlier version of "Net worth is nice, but self worth is even nicer," by Andrew Tobias, appeared in *We the People*, Rare Air Media, October 2000.

Production management: BookMatters
Book design: BookMatters
Cover design: Naylor Design

Library of Congress Cataloging-in-Publication Data

Why I'm a Democrat / edited by Susan Mulcahy ; foreword by David Brock.
    p. cm.
ISBN 13: 978-0-9794822-6-7
    1. Democratic Party (U.S.)—Miscellanea. 2. Democratic Party (U.S.)—Public opinion. 3. Public opinion—United States.
I. Mulcahy, Susan.
  JK2316.W49   2008
  324.273092'2—dc22   2008006695

Published by:
PoliPointPress, LLC
P.O. Box 3008
Sausalito, CA 94966-3008
(415) 339-4100
www.p3books.com

Distributed by Ingram Publisher Services

For Jeanne Grace Mulcahy,
who encouraged all six of her children to be good Democrats,
and Paul N. Mulcahy,
a Republican who is having second thoughts

Contents

Foreword

It was just a few years ago that bookshelves were stocked with volumes telling Democrats how they could pull themselves up out of their desperate political situation and begin to fight back against their Republican rivals. As E.J. Dionne wrote in one of those books, "The party that once galvanized a nation by declaring that there is nothing to fear but fear itself has become afraid—afraid of being too liberal, afraid of being weak on defense, afraid of being culturally permissive, afraid of being seen as apologizing for big government." But today, it is the conservative movement in disarray and the GOP wondering how it can hold itself together and fashion an appeal that the American public will not reject.

One can point to the effects of major national events and conditions as the explanation—the increasing inequality in our society, the skyrocketing cost of health care, or the myriad failures of the Bush administration, the most prominent of which is of course the Iraq war. But the real story of the Democratic revival is about ordinary Democrats.

They have given their party exactly what so many knew it needed: courage. The courage to fight its adversaries, and most of all, the courage of its convictions. People began organizing, in their hometowns and on the Internet, to provide the means and the backbone necessary to succeed. As always happens in politics, the politicians eventually got the message that the people were delivering, and success at the ballot box followed. I cannot recall a time in my life when Democrats were as organized, motivated, and effective as they are today, not simply as members of a party but as a movement.

Politics is a journey for all of us. The issues that dominate our national life when we are coming of age are radically different from those that demand our attention in our forties, fifties, and sixties. We try to find our way through those changes in the hope that what guides us is not some unreflective tribal allegiance but our most fundamental ideals. I happen to be one of the growing number of people who spent a long period among the conservatives but came to realize that they were on the wrong side.

For me, the process started when I began to understand the true character of the movement of which I had been a part. It's been said that Republicans claim that government is inherently incompetent and corrupt, and when they get a hold on that government, they set about to prove it. One might also say that Republicans believe that deep down we're all fundamentally bad, ready to descend into a Hobbesian nightmare of all against all—and when they campaign, they set about to prove it.

It would be foolish to claim that no Democrat has ever tossed an unfair attack or engaged in dirty tricks. It has happened in the past, and it will probably happen in the future. But as former Republican campaign operative Allen Raymond wrote, "When it came to playing in the gutter, we were the professionals—the Dems weren't even junior varsity." (Raymond went to prison for his role in the New Hampshire phone-jamming scandal, just one of the many recent GOP dirty-tricks operations.) Residing in the belly of the Republican beast, I saw the thirst for power unrestrained by any moral considerations, and it made me turn away in disgust.

But as my own journey proceeded, I realized that I was not merely fleeing something but moving toward something as well. I didn't become an Independent when I left the Republicans. I became a Democrat.

At its best, the Democratic Party has always been the party in which ordinary people could have their voices heard and their interests represented and in which each individual is honored for who they are. The stories in this book show Democrats at their best—people from all walks of life and with all kinds of personal histories who arrived at the same place because their beliefs demanded it. They join together to make their country a better place—that most patriotic of endeavors—finding in each other the wisdom and will that make change possible.

Like many Democrats, I like to refer to myself as a "progressive," because that term communicates not merely a laundry list of issue positions but the animating spirit that binds us together. The belief in progress—the faith that things can be better, that we can solve the problems that vex our nation, that though we will experience tragedies and setbacks the future is where our best days lie—makes a Democrat a Democrat. Republicans can be relied on to look backward, to argue that the answer to any current ill can be found in a return to an imagined Edenic past in which strict hierarchies were enforced and people knew their place, where shame and fear kept everyone in check. But Democrats are different.

It is no accident that there are so many kinds of people who call themselves Democrats, as the contributors to this book demonstrate so vividly. It was Democrats who led the civil rights movement, who led the women's rights movement, who led the environmental movement, and who today lead the movement for civil rights for gay Americans. Democrats are the crusaders for justice, the ones whose eyes are fixed on the future, the ones who work every day to maintain and enhance our nation's commitment to its founding ideals of equality and democracy.

That doesn't mean that Democratic politicians, and even the party as a whole, won't sometimes fail us. The temptations of timidity are strong, and power can eventually corrupt even the most well meaning. But the Democratic Party is indeed the party of the people, and the people will always have the power to make their party what they want it to be: strong, principled, hopeful, and committed. As long as they do, they can tell their stories with pride.

David Brock
President and CEO
Media Matters for America

Introduction

Why I'm a Democrat is a portrait of fifty-five people who have chosen to support the Democratic Party in the early years of the twenty-first century, and why. They express their views in essays, interviews, emails, lists, and artwork.

Although the book reflects the party's diversity, practical considerations keep it from being a wholly comprehensive portrait: by design I did not include politicians, political operatives, or anyone whose career is tied to politics, with two exceptions—a writer who is the treasurer of the Democratic National Committee, a job that pays one dollar a year; and a farmer who is a township trustee in Kansas, a part-time position in an area with about 250 registered voters. Though many participants are or have been active politically by working for candidates or campaigns—and in one case, thirty or so years ago, for a Republican congressman on Capitol Hill—just as many told me that, although they are Democrats, they are not particularly political. I said that was just fine. (In that, they are like most of us.)

The methodology I used for assembling the book's contributors was much like the party, a mixed bag. The idea was to ask a selected group of writers and artists to compose something illustrating their political affiliation, at the same time to interview Democrats from all over the country and all walks of life—some famous, some less well known. I attempted to include Democrats whose occupations are iconic or symbolic in some way—farmer, firefighter, teacher, doctor, diner waitress, Philly cheesesteak maker. At first, I planned to include members of the clergy— a rabbi, a nun, a Christian preacher—but decided that it was a lousy idea. Religion has received far too much emphasis in recent elections, so why encourage people who really should be impartial to take a political stand? Let them render unto Caesar in their own book. Several non-clerics ended up discussing their religious beliefs anyway.

In gathering the group of contributors, I was intent on examining stereotypes of the sort that declare all Cuban-Americans, or everyone in the rural West, or all Mormons to be Republicans. They're not. Many of the people with whom I spoke emphasized the Democratic Party's openness to all points of view. *Why I'm a Democrat* reflects that welcoming attitude—and even includes Democrats who don't much like the Democratic Party. I felt their stories were important, too. A few people I approached—whose opinions led me to believe they were Democrats—declined to participate. "What do you mean by Democrat? The party or the principle?" emailed one well-known novelist. "If I vote Democratic, it will only be because I despise the Republicans more, but most current so-called Democrats are equally despicable corporate puppets, with a very few exceptions." One high-tech CEO said he would take part only if the title of the book was changed to "Why I'm a Progressive." Well, neither life nor politics is that simple.

I didn't change the title, so he bowed out, but many progressive Democrats can be found within the pages of this book. Progressive principles *are* Democratic—as well as democratic, lower case *d*. Still, to be in the book, contributors had to declare membership in the party, upper case *D*, though I did include one individual who has lived in the United States for many years but is not a citizen. Residents not able to vote sometimes pay more attention to our political process than the legally eligible; during the 2004 presidential election, more than 70 million Americans who could have voted did not cast a ballot. (In that, they too, are like many of us.)

Many contributors commented on the inherent absurdity of a country with more than 300 million people being divided into only two viable political parties. Why can't we be more like France, they wondered, and have several? It is a good question, with many possible answers. I am not sure which is the most accurate, though I am willing to eat a lot of French fries while doing the research.

The 2000 elections showed the power of a third party to influence results—in a way few supporters of that third party could have imagined. Many now sorely regret their allegiance to Ralph Nader's presidential bid. A large portion of Nader voters—some of whom participated in this book—were Democrats. Eight years later, another pivotal election approaches. Despite a lingering sense on both the left and the right that the roots of the American spirit have been lost amid partisan rivalries, many disenfranchised Democrats have come back to the party, realizing that, like it or not, the United States is a two-party system and that the Democrats come closest to representing the ideals that define the American spirit.

The Democratic Party started as a congressional caucus in 1792 and in 1798 became the Democratic-Republican Party. (The name was later simplified.) In 1800 the party's founder, Thomas Jefferson, became its first winning presidential candidate. From the start the new party was seen as an alternative to the elitist Federalists, an image solidified thirty years later by the campaigns of Andrew Jackson. The modern Democratic Party emerged during the 1930s with Franklin D. Roosevelt's New Deal coalition. The Democrats are still widely considered the party of the worker, the union member, the so-called common man, even if in recent years many of those same working men and women ironically have voted for Republican candidates whose economic policies favor the wealthy. In a political culture dominated by personality, GOP candidates often win simply by acting, as one Democrat observed, like the kind of folks you'd enjoy having over for a barbecue. If George W. Bush ends up accomplishing anything, it may be that he helps shift the voting population's attention away from personal mythologies—the barbecue with no beef, as it were—and on to the things that matter.

Nearly eighty years ago, when my mother was a small child, she held my grandfather's hand as they stopped at a street corner in Fair Haven, Vermont, to let a funeral cortege pass. It is one of her earliest memories. As the hearse went by, my grandfather put his hat over his heart and commented, "He was a good Democrat. He'll be hard to replace."

A worthy epitaph.

Susan Mulcahy

Editor's Note: All entries in *Why I'm a Democrat* are original to this collection with two exceptions, Andrew Tobias's essay and William Wegman's drawing. Original entries by writers and artists were created during the second half of 2007, which is also when I conducted all interviews—over the phone, in person, or through email. All interviews have been edited for clarity and length. Some interview responses have been condensed into oral history–style entries, whereas other interviews appear in question-and-answer format.

★1★

The Party of a Lifetime

Democrats who have always been Democrats, and who say they are unlikely to change, do not conform to any particular pattern or lifestyle. Some eat hamburgers. Some are vegan. Some wear double-breasted suits to the office, while others don different sorts of uniforms. Still others work from home and others, from the stage of concert halls. These Democrats may originally have registered as the result of a specific influence, but after a certain amount of time, having experienced what it means to be a Democrat, they can't imagine being anything else; for them *Democrat* is more than a political designation. Though they recognize that occasionally, elected Democrats may not act in accordance with their own beliefs on a specific issue, they do not abandon their commitment to the party. At its core, the Democratic Party stands for the same principles that guide them personally. Many contributors to *Why I'm a Democrat* fall into this category. Following is a selective sample.

Irma Thomas

Louisiana

Irma Thomas, long recognized as the "Soul Queen of New Orleans," has been performing and recording for nearly fifty years. She won a Grammy Award for Best Contemporary Blues Album in 2007 for *After the Rain*. Thomas moved back to New Orleans in April 2007 after being forced from her home in the wake of Hurricane Katrina.

Was politics part of your family life growing up?

You have to remember that I'm sixty-six years old. When I was young, it was a time of segregation, when blacks were not even allowed to vote. By the time I came of age, that was when they used to put black people through a lot of changes to vote, to keep them from having a voice in the voting machine.

So when did you first vote?

Soon as I came of age. I had to go through a battery of questions to register, sort of trick questions. We had gone through a class with some folks from the NAACP who were training people interested in becoming registered voters. We'd make sure to read the instructions very carefully, because there were trick questions like, "I (have, have not) been arrested?" or I (have, have not) been in jail." You had to be careful to scratch out the right thing or it would read that you had been to jail.

Did you register as a Democrat?
I sure did.

Why?
Because it was a Democrat who took the time to teach me how to vote—a young man who was part of the NAACP program. They brought people to the South to those places where black people were having difficulty getting registered. It cost some people their lives. I registered during the time we were fighting for the right to be equal citizens.

Who was the first presidential candidate who impressed you?
Kennedy.

What was it about him?
Even as a young person I had the innate ability to judge people just from the way they carried themselves and the way they spoke. And he didn't give me the impression that he was talking out of the sides of his mouth. Everything that he said he meant it sincerely; he took chances on speaking up for the rights of everybody as opposed to just whites, or just blacks. He stood for the right thing to do, and it was the right Christian thing to do, and he left me with that.

What do you think of the way certain Republicans use the Christian religion to further political movements?
First of all, I think that, Republican or Democrat, they're gonna say what they think people want to hear to get them to vote. Whether Republican or Democrat, they're politicians.

Is there any one word or phrase that you would use to describe a Democrat?

Most of the Democrats that I've paid any attention to have believed in trying to help people *in general,* not just some, not just others, but in general. Especially as a senior citizen, I'm concerned about those who are fighting for the rights of people to have a quality of life in their old age. Even though I'm a Democrat, I'm not gonna always agree with what the Democrats are saying. I look at the person. I probably won't ever vote Republican, but by the same token I'm still gonna pay attention to those folks, to what they are saying—and what they are *not* saying—and vote for the person that has said the things that I think, that I feel, are genuine.

Have you ever campaigned for a Democratic politician?

I don't openly campaign for any of 'em. A lot of politicians who live in this area grew up listening to my music. They hire me to do their campaign parties, both Democrat and Republican. Fortunately they understand that they don't put me on the carpet and ask me, "Are you a Republican or a Democrat?" I'm the drawing card to get people in there and do some fundraising, so they don't question me on my voting status, and I wouldn't tell them anyway.

So you're a bipartisan entertainer?

That's right.

Nora Ephron

New York

Nora Ephron is a journalist, novelist, playwright, screenwriter, and director. Her credits include *Heartburn*, *When Harry Met Sally*, *Sleepless in Seattle*, *You've Got Mail*, and *Imaginary Friends*. Her latest book, *I Feel Bad About My Neck: And Other Thoughts on Being a Woman*, is a number one best seller. She lives in New York City.

Ten reasons why I'm a Democrat:

1. My parents were Democrats.
2. I am deeply in love with some abstract concept called FDR.
3. The Democratic Party stands for everything I stand for, even though I'm not sure exactly where that Democratic Party is (in reality), but it's definitely still in existence in my imagination. It believes that government exists to make life better for its citizens, in an activist way.
4. I have never voted for a Republican.
5. I barely know a Republican.

6. The Supreme Court.
7. The Supreme Court.
8. The Supreme Court.
9. The Supreme Court.
10. The Supreme Court.

Hannah Sessions

Vermont

Hannah Sessions, of Blue Ledge Farm in Leicester, Vermont, is a goat dairy farmer and cheese maker. She and her husband have a mixed herd of Nubian, Alpine, and LaMancha goats and make six kinds of goat cheese.

What do you expect from the Democratic Party in return for your vote?

I expect some great programs to continue. Vermont has an incredible program called Doctor Dinosaur, which offers health care to all children. Governor Howard Dean installed that program. I would expect it to continue to be a priority, along with education. My husband and I are loyal Democrats because we were able to start our business with the help of Democratic programs. For one thing, our children have health insurance through the state, and there is no way we could ever have taken the plunge without that. The State of Vermont is a liberally run state, and it really encourages small businesses in a lot of ways.

Are you from a farm family?

My parents weren't farmers, but most of my mom's cousins are dairy farmers, and my grandmother's family goes back eight generations farming in Vermont. So that would make me tenth generation.

Was politics part of the family discourse when you were growing up?

Very much so. I remember campaigning when I was seven, walking around neighborhoods handing out leaflets for a local state representative here in Vermont. My dad, who's a lawyer, chaired Senator Leahy's campaign one year. When I was seven or eight I received an autographed book from Geraldine Ferraro. It was her autobiography. On the inside it said, "Hannah, the election of '84 was for you." That was very thrilling for me. I also remember making a banner out of fabric, like a small quilt, and going down to Washington with my family. We formed a chain around the Pentagon with the banners. Every family had made one. They were about peace and nonproliferation and that sort of thing. It was in 1986, so I was probably about ten.

Did you know as a child that when you were getting involved in these political activities with your parents it was as a Democrat?

Yes.

And what did that mean?

It was sort of a family joke. When I was a kid, my parents would say, "You can marry anyone as long as he is not a Republican." But we have many friends who are Republican, so it was mostly talk.

Did you marry a Republican?

I did marry someone who voted for Bob Dole, yes. He has since converted. I think he may even have converted before we married. But Bob Dole was a pretty nice Republican.

What is the political situation in Vermont in the farm community?

There is a real divide right now. The larger, more conventional farmers tend to be Republicans. The newer farmers, such as ourselves, who are smaller or alternative, they are oftentimes Democrats.

What do the larger farmers get out of being Republicans?

Well, I think a lot of them are Jim Jeffords Republicans, Republicans of a bygone era. Some of it has to do with their parents being Republicans, a nostalgia for the past. Or maybe they are antiregulation in terms of pollution controls on their farms.

There is a stereotypical perception of New Englanders, of Yankees, as being completely independent.

Vermont is a fascinating political scene. We oftentimes have a Republican governor, but we always seem to elect Democrats to go to Washington for us. Vermonters really vote on the likeability of a candidate, and on their honor. Bernie [Sanders—Independent U.S. Senator who has described himself as a democratic socialist] is such an interesting figure. He is very popular among the most liberal people and among many Republicans as well. He's a working-class guy with messy hair. Sometimes people don't like how polished Democrats can be. That would be the one thing that I don't like about the Democratic Party is that they can be very "PC," very polished. I think it's the one thing we can learn from George Bush. You appeal to people when you just talk to them, when people want to have you over to their barbecue. That's why Al Gore lost. People didn't really like him. The likability factor is huge in Vermont.

But the truth is that George Bush is not a down-home guy. He summered in Kennebunkport and went to Yale. His image is a highly polished version of something unpolished.

It's true, but that façade works better for a lot of people.

Is there a book or a movie or a song that says "Democrat" to you?

Anything by Bruce Springsteen.

Can you define "Democrat"?

I came across a bumper sticker once that said, "We all do better when we're all doing better." That sums it all up for me. It's the idea that humanity is at its best when we can look out for each other, even for people we never have met and probably never will meet.

Thomas Lauderdale

Oregon

Thomas Lauderdale, a pianist, is founder and artistic director of Pink Martini, the twelve-piece "little orchestra" based in Portland, Oregon, whose third album, *Hey Eugene*, was released in 2007.

Why am I a Democrat? Do I have a choice?

Pink Martini was born out of Democratic politics. When I was in high school, I worked for Portland mayor Bud Clark, I served on a couple of commissions under Oregon's governor Neil Goldschmidt, and I worked on the city's civil rights ordinance under City Commissioner Gretchen Kafoury. I really thought I would go into politics instead of music.

When I came back to Oregon in 1994 after graduating from Harvard, I went "straight" into the fight against a really nasty anti-gay ballot initiative in Oregon—Measure 13. Parenthetically, I had just seen *Pee Wee Herman's Christmas Special* with every guest star imaginable—Oprah Winfrey, Frankie Avalon and Annette Funicello, Whoopi Goldberg, Zsa Zsa Gabor, Dinah Shore, k.d. lang, Grace Jones . . . and the Del Rubio Triplets, three gals, somewhere between seventy and eighty years old, who played their guitars and sang covers of "Walk Like an Egyptian" and "Whip It." They were fabulous. So I called them. I found them in the phone book. I thought it would be great to have them perform at nursing homes and hospitals and retirement homes and sneak in a "No on 13" message at the end, which they did. At the end of the week, we did a big public fundraising concert, but I needed an opening act. I couldn't get hold of the surf band, Satan's Pilgrims, so I threw on a cocktail dress, found a singer, a bass player, and a bongo boy, and that's how Pink Martini started. It was supposed to be a one-time thing, but it took off and soon we soon found ourselves performing at all kinds of fundraisers for progressive causes—affordable housing, the environment, public libraries. The same kind of Democratic principles that brought this country the WPA [Works Progress Administration] projects, Social Security, civil rights, a woman's right to choose—that sense of fairness, equality, righting wrongs, recognizing that we are not all given the same opportunities—are so in keeping with the activism of the band.

The idea was to create a beautiful, fabulous atmosphere for these progressive fundraisers, a sort of Breakfast-at-Tiffany's-meets-the-United-Nations kind of band, with a multilingual repertoire drawing upon various traditions of symphonic, jazz, and world music.

We are not an overtly political band, but I do think we are inherently political. We play all over the world and throughout the United States, and we often play in very conservative communities in the United States. The closest thing we have to a protest song is "To a Little Radio," an antiwar song composed by Hanns Eisler and Bertolt Brecht in Germany in the early 1930s. We introduce it as such, with varying results in the United States and to cheers abroad. All one has to do is say "antiwar" and you lose a few people, but I think all of us in the band feel a huge commitment here and abroad to try to undo some of the incredible damage done by the current administration. We played Beirut in 2000. The current administration has made this practically impossible. Being from Portland, Oregon—dubbed "Little Beirut" by George Bush the First—it seemed like a good idea to record a song in Arabic for our third album. So in a sense that's partially a protest song, too.

I think our music is very Democratic. It represents the real diversity and complexity that is America. As the most hetero-geneously populated country in the entire world, comprised of people of all nations, religions, cultures, languages, traditions, it's important to remember that none of us are really from here—we are all mutts. China Forbes, the lead singer (and cousin of John Kerry), and I are both multiracial. She's Scottish-French-African-American, and I'm half Caucasian and half mystery Asian—I was adopted so I'm not sure exactly. The music we write and perform articulates and accurately reflects the complexity of real America in 2008.

James Brady

New York

James Brady, who lives in Manhattan and East Hampton, writes weekly for *Parade* magazine and for Forbes.com. His most recent book is the nonfiction *Why Marines Fight*.

"Silent Cal" Coolidge was president when I was born in November 1928, but Herbert Hoover had just defeated Al Smith in the election, and in my Irish American family in Sheepshead Bay, Brooklyn, there was resentment over the anti-Catholic bias and mudslinging tone of the Hoover win. Smith, if elected, would take his orders from the pope. That sort of antediluvian swift-boating rubbish.

In a neighborhood where aproned mothers rushed out to sweep up innocent children from the stoops of row houses if a Republican walked by, it was soon clear that I, too, was expected as a Catholic to be for the Democrats. By the time I was in my teens I understood Roosevelt always had been and always would be President, and rightly so. As a college boy in a Catholic school I was tossed out of a speech class for declaiming politely against Senator Joe McCarthy as a demagogue. After class the Neanderthal teacher privately urged me to pray to the Holy Spirit on grounds I was well on my way to joining the Commies and losing my soul, attacking a noble Catholic like McCarthy.

In 1948 I turned twenty, still too young to vote for either Truman or Dewey. The Korean War began eighteen months later and I went to it. It was, for combat Marine infantrymen like me, an apolitical war. We were vaguely aware that General MacArthur was already politicking for the Republican nomination in 1952 and that Truman was increasingly unpopular. We disliked Truman because he'd slighted the Marines as publicity hounds, but we hated MacArthur because of his bloody handling of the Corps during the Pacific War and more recently, how he nearly lost the First Marine Division in a Red Chinese trap in North Korea, which he had arrogantly refused to recognize as a threat. The only politician I saw in Korea was a visiting Republican senator named Homer Ferguson, when I was ordered to muster any of his state's men in my platoon to meet their senator. I was only a twenty-three-year-old lieutenant but understood this sort of bullshit.

I came home the summer of 1952, ready to cast my first ballot in an election. Stevenson caught my imagination, an articulate, even thrilling orator and an intelligent and thoughtful fellow, but Ike was enormously popular. The voting wasn't even close. I was writing ad copy for Macy's, and my friend Ab Gomberg and I went over to Times Square to follow the returns on the news ribbon. "This is rough as a cob," Gomberg said, as the increasingly Republican lead grew. But I had voted for the first time. And for a Democrat.

By the mid-1950s, I was covering the Senate as a Washington correspondent for Fairchild Publications. On election night I was assigned to the Shoreham Hotel, GOP headquarters, a pretty sad occasion. The admirable Stevenson had lost even worse. Eisenhower—by now to me an inarticulate, plodding fellow—

came out with Mamie to take a bow. His voice was thick, his diction blurred. My God, I thought, he's drunk. Up in the balcony where we were stationed, veteran reporters scoffed. Then Richard and Pat Nixon joined the Eisenhowers onstage. The Republicans went nuts. I wrote the scene, though not about the president's poor performance (probably a leftover from an earlier minor stroke), which went unmentioned.

It was embarrassing to attend Eisenhower speeches, which were wooden and less eloquent even than those of the Third World leaders, who spoke before joint sessions of the Congress. A thug like Indonesia's Sukarno came to town and brilliantly quoted Jefferson while Ike plodded through his prepared remarks. But it was also during my three years on Capitol Hill as a young and relatively unimportant reporter that I developed a reluctant disillusionment with some of my liberal heroes. Senator Paul Douglas of Illinois turned out surly; Herbert Lehman of New York, dull and ponderous; Lyndon Johnson was brilliant but capable of cruelty and vulgarity; Wayne Morse was sour tempered; many of the Southerners, while courteous and gregarious, were clearly racist. While Nixon the vice-president was odious—and Joe McCarthy, by now censured, was often drunk, as was another Republican, Herman Welker, of Idaho—other members of the GOP provided sharp contrast. Barry Goldwater, politically unpalatable to a young New Yorker of liberal bent, was one of the most gracious, thoughtful, and civilized men on the Hill. Right-wing dinosaur Bill Jenner was amiable, generous with his time, and patient with a reporter. Leverett Saltonstall of Massachusetts was a gentleman. Jack Javits seemed to speak my language.

I got to know John Kennedy, and even better, his kid brother Bobby, counsel to an investigating committee on which I was a beat reporter. I attended LBJ's daily noon briefings on the Senate floor. The whole thing was a civics lesson I was getting paid for.

Then it was to Europe to work the correspondent's trade for the next six years, and a civics lesson of a different sort—House of Parliament sessions, how prime ministers, on their feet and without notes, handled sometimes hostile "question times," the Budget day I saw Churchill—fat, old, and deaf—totter in. In France, de Gaulle was monarchal, impressively quick on his feet; Andre Malraux, cynical, shrewd, chain-smoking, all facial tics and energy, the Minister of Culture welcoming a young American reporter in his chambers at the Palais Royal.

In 1960 I cast my vote for Kennedy by absentee ballot from Paris, but I was back in New York, as the publisher of *Women's Wear Daily*, in 1964. The election that year pitted Goldwater against a sitting President Johnson. My politics were Johnson's, but I knew Goldwater to be a more decent fellow. How do we vote, for the policy or the man? Politics won out, rather easily in that case, and I pulled the Democratic lever again.

All of this happened years and decades ago, and I am still, though sometimes skeptically, a Democrat. Nothing that has happened during two terms of George Bush's absurd and often foolish presidency has persuaded me to change parties.

James Naughton

Connecticut

James Naughton is a stage, film, and television actor and director. He has won Tony awards for performances in *Chicago* and *City of Angels*, and has appeared in *The Devil Wears Prada*, *Factory Girl*, and many other films, and on such television programs as *Law & Order* and *Ally McBeal*. His directing credits include the recent Broadway revivals of *Our Town* and *The Price*.

Did you ever think about any other sort of affiliation—say, registering as an Independent?

I never had any inclination to do anything like that. It did not make any sense to me. It just meant I would not have the opportunity to vote in the primaries. I think sometimes people have a hard time making up their minds, and that is what being Independent is about. That's not the case for me. Too often people have an allegiance to a party that is like being a fan of a sports team. It blinds them to the relative merits of an argument. Or they say they vote for the person. But, for example, while I respect John McCain for a lot of things, I couldn't vote for him because he's had the third most conservative voting record while he's been in the Senate.

Why are you a Democrat?

The Democrats identify with and are for the common man, the working man. While I think our form of capitalist democracy is about the best form of government that has been devised, it clearly needs to be regulated to prevent abuses. If you are for smaller government, and the Republicans seem to be, then you are not for regulation. That's one reason. Aside from that, the Democrats practice tolerance, and the Republicans do not. The Republicans want to restrict behavior, belief, and that kind of thing. Their attitude is: it's my way or the highway.

Can you think of one incident or experience that has validated your decision to be a Democrat?

I see it every time I pick up the paper. I can think of only one thing Bush has done in seven years that I agree with—his position on immigration—but his party killed him on it. I can't think of another issue where I agreed with him.

Can you think of a film or a song that says "Democrat" to you?

Not off the top of my head, although maybe Pete Seeger's music, or "Brother, Can You Spare a Dime?"—that sort of thing. One experience I recall does. When I was in college in the 1960s—I was at Brown and lived in Fox Point, the old section of Providence—I was talking to a local guy. When he worked, he was a longshoreman, but work was hard to find. He was black. He had a little boy named Stevie. My roommate and I used to take Stevie skating. It was 1964 or 1965. I was telling his father not to despair, that things were changing; landmark [civil rights] legislation was about to be enacted. He said, "Jimmy, you know my boy Stevie. It's not going to happen in time for Stevie, is it?" I thought about it, and I had to say, no, it's not. Stevie was probably four years old, growing up in the tough part of town, with a father who was present, but unemployed. By the time the laws were actually enacted and put into effect and had trickled down to the local level, Stevie was going to miss it. It's one thing to mouth platitudes, but when it comes right down to it, these things have a cost. That was a meaningful exchange for me.

What do you expect in return for your vote?

One of the things that has happened in the last eight or ten years is this tremendous separation between the classes. The rich just seem to get richer. The separation has gotten embarrassingly large. I would look for the Democrats to enact legislation to try and rectify that.

Maira Kalman

New York

Maira Kalman, whose work appears regularly in the *New Yorker*
and the *New York Times*, has also written and illustrated twelve
children's books. Other recent projects include *The Elements of
Style* (illustrated) and an illustrated memoir, *The Principles of
Uncertainty*.

I
AM
A
DEMOCRAT.

BECAUSE I HAVE A
SENSE OF HUMOR!
AND A LOVE
OF PEOPLE! AND
DEMOCRACY!
And STRAWBERRY
CheeseCAKE! and A
LOVE OF SPINOZA!
MAIRA KALMAN

★2★

The Helpful Party

Gradually, then all of a sudden over the past few decades, supporting those in need went out of fashion. So did kindness. Nastiness infiltrated everything from humor—which became sharper edged and more cynical—to business—where the tough but fair-minded CEO, possibly played by Spencer Tracy, was replaced by Gordon Gekko and his rapacious descendents. During the Reagan Revolution, people came to believe that all government was bad and that any money collected in taxes would be frittered away on corruption and bureaucracies. The Great Communicator himself made an ironic joke of the phrase, "I'm from the government and I'm here to help." Recent generations have criticized or even forgotten the great social investments of the preceding ones: Social Security, unemployment compensation, Medicaid and Medicare, Aid to Dependent Children, rural electrification, the Works Progress Administration (WPA). Even such grand collective efforts as building the Interstate Freeway System and putting a man on the moon have come under scrutiny. While the problems facing Americans in an age of technology and globalization call for different solutions than those developed in the past, for Democrats, the essential impulse has not changed. They still believe that helping people in need is the right thing to do—even, or especially, when it appears to be out of style.

Isaac Mizrahi

New York

Isaac Mizrahi is the winner of three Designer of the Year awards from the Council of Fashion Designers of America. He designs clothing and accessories for better department stores, and in January 2008 was named creative director of the Liz Claiborne brand. He also designs costumes for stage and film, appears regularly on stage and TV, and is the host of his own online program at isaacmizrahiny.com.

Why are you a Democrat?

Because I'm not mean and selfish enough to be a Republican.

How did your parents vote?

They were Democrats because they were New Yorkers, and they were smart.

Did you pay attention to politics growing up?

A little. When I was in grade school, I worked for McGovern. You had to pick a side in eighth grade, and do—airquote—"campaigning" for McGovern. So, I—airquote—"campaigned." I remember there were buttons involved and I had some input into designing the graphics. I was a devoted McGovern fan. I watched him on TV.

What did you like about him?

He seemed to have a sense of what was good. He floundered in the face of greatness. I like people who are good. I don't like people who are great. Great is a result. Good is what you do every day. It's a process. If there is something greater than something else, you have to have a war over it. If you are living for greatness, don't bother. When it's all over, and you're dead and gone, somebody may say you're great, but who cares?

What do you think of Republicans, vis-à-vis greatness?

The Republicans tell you that they are great, in advance of doing the most horrible things in the world. Democrats say, "Here is what I will try and do—the right thing, the good thing."

Do you have any Republican friends?

Of course. I have all kinds of friends. In fact, one of my friends is a Republican who is pro-gun. It's a source of terrible friction between us. I love her, but it does take a great deal of effort to be friends, knowing how she feels.

What do you do when you are at a dinner party and you realize everyone else is a Republican?

That's happened to me. I say, "What am I doing here?" I got into an argument once at a party like that. The other guests said, "Well, don't you want to protect your rights to pay less taxes?" and I said, "No, I would not." I'm not that selfish. Not *everyone* thinks only about himself. A certain kind of Republican says: to hell with the rest of the earth as long as I can have air conditioning. I say: if it would save the earth, why don't we live without air conditioning?

Dave Dederer

Washington

Dave Dederer is a founding member (guitarist and vocals) of the Grammy-nominated rock band The Presidents of the United States of America. He is also the vice president of media content at Melodeo, a Seattle-based developer of web and mobile audio and video distribution.

I'm a Democrat:

Because I'm already enough of an asshole.

Because it's usually easy to be the lowest-scoring Dem in your foursome.

Because there's absolutely nothing rock-and-roll about being a Republican, a point made all the more clear by lame attempts to prove otherwise (Lee Atwater, anyone?).

Because we do better with the ladies. President Clinton or President Kennedy versus any Republican president—*ever*—in a singles' night grudge match. Who walks away with more phone numbers? You call that a contest?

Because I briefly met President Clinton in 1995 and once he has measured your soul with his piercing blue eyes and engulfed your hand in his elegant, long fingers, you are done for and will be a card-carrying liberal for at least five lifetimes.

Because at least we *pretend* to care.

Because in the early nineties I volunteered at Seattle's juvenile detention center and saw firsthand the havoc wrought by the twelve years of Reagan and Bush administration budget cuts to social services.

All other reasons being facetious, moot, or inadequate, I offer these three words: civil rights movement.

Ronald Davenport Sr.

Pennsylvania

Ronald Davenport Sr. is chairman of Sheridan Broadcasting Corporation, based in Pittsburgh, and a former dean of the Duquesne University School of Law. He has served on numerous civic and corporate boards, including the National Board of the United States Chamber of Commerce, and the National Urban League Board of Directors.

Have you always been a Democrat?

I have, but at times, I supported Republicans—John Heinz, for one.

Was politics part of your life growing up?

Politics was always part of my interests. I was active in high school government, and in college, as well. My generation in general is one that believed in public service, not in the sense of serving at soup kitchens—more governmental service. We believed in taking the skills and talents we had to make the world a better place—to make our cities and our country a better place.

When did you first think of yourself as a Democrat?

In my day, you couldn't register until you were twenty-one. I always believed that the Democratic values were more consistent with who I was.

What were those values?

The distribution of the most goods and services to the most people. The Democrats had a better view and a better understanding of that. They still stand for that. The whole issue of social values at times has overwhelmed the public's sense of what is in its best interest. Often people vote for candidates on an emotional basis rather than thinking through what programs would be best for them. That's what led to the rise of the Reagan Democrats at a time when we had a strong economy and people were not concerned with keeping their jobs. The idea that the wealthy should have low taxes . . . I believe in a progressive tax structure that encourages the creation of wealth because I don't think socialism works, but those of us who do well have a responsibility to make sure there is a real safety net. There has been a dismantling of the social safety net since the Reagan years. I think that recent elections show that the Reagan Democrats are coming home. They are losing their jobs. They're asking, who is going to protect us?

Who was the first candidate you felt passionate about?

Kennedy, but I didn't vote for him. I would have voted for him, but I was in the hospital with a ruptured appendix. I was in law school at the time. It happened about a week before the election.

Did you work for him?

I canvassed for voters. And I was very active with the NAACP. I headed their Legal Defense Fund office in Mississippi in 1964.

I worked on the Cleve McDowell case. He was the student kicked out of Ole Miss [University of Mississippi] Law School for carrying a gun, which he sorely needed.

What would you say to Democrats who are disillusioned with the party?

My question would be: what are the alternatives? I always remember Will Rogers saying he didn't belong to an organized party, he belonged to the Democrats. We are thoughtful and fair. The Democrats bring a sense of honesty and fairness to the process. The Republicans have more of a singleness of purpose. They try to put a nonpartisan face on partisan activities.

How would you suggest the Democrats go about bringing more voters back to the party?

I think the answer is honesty, being able to communicate. St. Thomas Aquinas said, if you are going to persuade a man, you must first go to where he is and bring him to you. Talk *to* people, not at them. You can't preach at people and tell them what they should be doing. You have to say: what are your interests? People are not stupid.

Thomas Christopher Erkelens

Utah

T.C. Erkelens, who was born and raised in Salt Lake City, recently completed a masters of science degree in sociology at Utah State University. He is a seminary teacher for The Church of Jesus Christ of Latter-Day Saints (LDS) in Ogden, Utah.

What do you teach?

Religion. Kids going to public school—it's grades nine to twelve—get permission from their parents to leave school for an hour to come to an adjacent LDS seminary to take my class. It's scripture study.

Are there a lot of Mormon Democrats?

Most Mormons are Republicans, usually because of social conservative reasons.

What would those be?

Abortion, gay marriage. Also, welfare—people depending on government versus being independent. Those kinds of issues.

But you're a Democrat. Why?

My own personal reasons for being a Democrat have to do with what I read in scripture about the life of Christ. His life was all about helping people and taking care of people. When I would look at politics, it seemed to me that Republicans were mostly against helping people, and Democrats were pushing for laws to help people. I liked that stance—trying to find solutions for people's problems, not trying to make life more difficult for them. Helping the poor and that kind of thing. It fits with what I've learned from reading about Christ. Another thing that made me a Democrat is the fact that I like our environment. I think God created the earth for us and made us its stewards. It's our responsibility to take care of it and use it wisely. Again, Republican policies always seem to be anti-environment. It boggles my mind that people would not want to take care of this place where we live.

Do you have LDS friends who are Democrats?

I do. Not a lot. But we get together and talk. There's a guy I teach with. He's been a Republican. He actually served as party chair of his county. We've talked a lot. He's more and more frustrated with what is happening with the Republican Party, with the kind of things I mentioned. He's asking himself: Why am I part of a party that doesn't want to help kids get health insurance? Why am I part of a party that supports the use of torture as an interrogation technique? He's been thinking hard about those issues.

Did you do a mission for the church?

I served a mission when I was nineteen, in Argentina.

How did that inform your politics?

Going to South America, you see a lot of poverty. From that experience, I looked at being a citizen of the United States very differently. In some cases, I saw a United States with policies that took advantage of other countries. Democrats seem less likely to have those kinds of policies. Republicans sometimes look to make America better at the expense of other countries.

Enid Duany Mendoza

Florida

Enid Mendoza is a partner with the law firm of Colson Hicks Eidson in Coral Gables, Florida.

When did you become a Democrat?

I left Cuba in 1960 and grew up in Barcelona, Spain, under the totalitarian Franco regime. I came to the United States in 1969 as a college student, married an American, and became a citizen in the mid-1970s. I registered as a Democrat.

Why?

My grandmother was probably the most influential person in my life. She was the daughter of one of the people who started the Cuban revolution against Spain in the 1860s. Carlos Manuel de Céspedes, who in Cuba is like George Washington, was her uncle. Her grandfather was caught running arms into Cuba under an American flag and was killed by a firing squad. She was a liberal and pounded liberalism into us. She believed government should take care of people.

How would you define "Democrat"?

It's government helping the people, reaching down to the less unfortunate.

How did your experience in Spain influence your politics?

It showed me what a lack of freedom of speech and a heavy hand could do.

Was your grandmother in Spain with you?

No, that was in the United States. She came here after the Bay of Pigs.

Why do you think so many Cuban Americans are Republicans? Is it still over the Bay of Pigs?

That's not quite accurate. I think that Cubans feel that President Kennedy disappointed them by not providing air coverage during the Bay of Pigs. But that wasn't the only reason the Bay of Pigs failed, and that's not the only reason some Cubans are Republicans. I will tell you a funny story about political affiliation and my family. I gave birth to a daughter the day after Reagan was elected in 1980, November fifth. By that time, I had been married seven years. When my brothers-in-law came to see me at the hospital, we started talking about the election. It was at that time that my husband found out that I was a Democrat. He is a conservative Republican. He couldn't believe I had been canceling his vote all those years.

Has he switched in the years since?

No, but he voted for Clinton twice, and he's threatening to vote for a Democrat the next time, too. I will tell you something else: the law firm where I work is small, fifteen lawyers. Half are Democrats and half are Republicans. Our top partners are important leaders in both the Democratic and Republican parties here. And everybody gets along.

Jon Elliott

California

Before becoming a radio host, Jon Elliott, who is based in San Diego, spent more than thirty years as a business executive, including as CEO of the Royal Casino Group. His nationally syndicated program, *This is America*, is heard Monday through Friday on stations throughout the country.

So many talk-radio hosts are Republicans. How does a Democrat end up in that line of work?

For that very reason! Back in 2002 there was a significant under-representation of liberal talk-show hosts. Actually, there were none. So I thought, here is an opportunity to bring balance to the airwaves. With the Republicans exhibiting dangerous behavior, I believed *someone* needed to tell the other side to the other side, and I decided I would.

How do Democratic talk-show hosts differ?

For the most part we're members of the reality-based community. Truth is mostly MIA from conservative hosts' playbooks. Another huge difference between liberal and conservative hosts is that we will criticize our own team when we believe they are wrong. I will frequently rail on Democrats when they back down on an issue—and on their leadership if they fail to bring a measure to a vote because they're afraid of splitting their own party. (Of course, I rarely miss an opportunity to rant about the wayward activities of Republicans. And there have been *so* many to choose from.) On the other hand, conservative hosts will *always* excuse or attempt to explain away even the most egregious actions by Republicans.

Of all the ideals at the foundation of the Democratic Party, what is the most important to you and why?

The unwavering determination to seek fairness for all Americans.

Can you tell me the specifics of an incident that happened to you at any point in your life that made you say, "That's why I'm a Democrat!"

I was raised in Canada by a mother who was a Democrat. Actually, she was a member of Canada's Liberal Party, but it's a mirror image of the Democrats. If you're a Liberal in Canada, you're essentially a Democrat. Also, we got much of our news from American television, and we studied American history in school. So I knew all about the Kennedys and was fascinated by them. I wondered why brothers born into unlimited wealth and privilege actually cared about . . . people like me? When I saw that they were dedicating themselves to making the lives of everyone better, I said, "I want to be a part of that!" Later, when I moved to the United States, I did become part of it by joining the Democrats.

Other than the Kennedys and your mother, can you name anyone else who inspired you to be a Democrat?

Lester Pearson. Again, he was Canadian, the leader of the Liberal Party throughout most of my formative years. He instituted many

policies designed to enhance the lives of all citizens. For his dip-
lomatic efforts, he was awarded the Nobel Peace Prize. Liberal in
Canada, or Democrat in the United States, it's really the same. It's
a moral thing, an integrity thing. It's caring about all people having access to the basics of a good life.

Roz Chast

Connecticut

Roz Chast is a staff cartoonist for the *New Yorker*. She has written or illustrated more than a dozen books, including *Theories of Everything: Selected, Collected, and Health-Inspected Cartoons, 1978–2006* and *The Alphabet from A to Y with Bonus Letter Z!*, a collaboration with comedian Steve Martin.

★3★

The Party of Liberty and Other Essentials

The Declaration of Independence, the U.S. Constitution, and the Bill of Rights get so much lip service in political contests, you would think that all candidates, and voters, had actually read them. For those who have, certain passages stand out. Like the Declaration of Independence, which declares all Americans to be created equal and "endowed by their Creator with certain unalienable Rights." Or the Fourteenth Amendment on the rights of naturalized citizens. And, especially, the First Amendment, with its clause prohibiting Congress from making laws "abridging the freedom of speech." Democrats appreciate the efforts of the founders of the United States—and other leaders who later expanded upon the truths espoused in the original documents—to make certain we all have the freedom to live honestly and openly, the opportunity to achieve professional and personal goals despite humble backgrounds, and the right to state opinions without fear of retribution. And they feel that of the two dominant parties, the Democrats are more likely to uphold these rights and protect those freedoms.

Tony Bennett

New York

Tony Bennett is one of the most successful entertainers in history. He has sold more than 50 million records worldwide, and is the recipient of fifteen Grammy Awards, two Emmy Awards, and is a Kennedy Center Honoree and an NEA Jazz Master. Bennett's passion for the arts—he is also a world-renowned painter—led him to found Exploring the Arts (ETA), a nonprofit organization that supports and funds arts education in public schools. He is also the founder of the Frank Sinatra School of the Arts, a New York City public arts high school, located in his hometown of Queens.

Why are you a Democrat?

FDR. I grew up during the Depression and I have stayed a Democrat my whole life. My dad died when I was very young and my mother had to raise three children. She was a seamstress. She worked for a penny a dress. I could not believe the way the Hoover administration left everybody so stranded. I have never gotten over that. I know times change, but not really. I am against super-greed. I am not an Ayn Rand fan. I have always believed that the Democrats at least work toward making things fair for everyone. Now we're being told the Democratic politicians are as bad as

51

the Republicans. I do not believe that. I think all the potential Democratic nominees are very good. Whoever gets in, I would feel more comfortable with than the government we have now.

Why?

Because the Democrats keep reminding everybody of the Constitution. What our forefathers created was genius, and the Democrats know that. Another thing that is shocking to me right now is this carelessness about the middle class. As a performer, these are the people I have met over the years, these wonderful Americans. When there's a middle class, it makes everybody feel that they have hope, that they might have that kind of life. The most important thing is to give people back hope. During times like the Roosevelt regime, or the Kennedy years, there was hope. Now we're being told it's too expensive to have a middle class in this country. I'm an entertainer and I travel around the world. I've seen countries where the rich have all the assets, and the majority of the people are so poor they're just struggling to survive. We don't want to see that happen here.

Of the ideals that are the basis for the Democratic Party, which is the most important?

Getting back to the Constitution. Giving the country back to the people. Everybody forgets that if we pay taxes, we are more powerful than the president and the vice president and the Congress and the Senate. We own this country. The public owns the country. But the government has stopped listening to what we want. This is such an important time. It is so important that the Democrats get back in next year.

What else would you like to see change?

I became a pacifist because of the war. I was in the infantry in France and Germany in World War II. We won that one, and it was still very tough. I know just where they're at, these soldiers. What I would like to see is our troops coming home. I can't wait until we bring them all home.

A few years ago, the United Nations made me a world citizen. Because I travel all over the world, I realize that on this planet earth, everybody is important, not just the United States. Luckily, the rest of the world loves America's citizens, but not our leaders. We used to be envied all over the world, but now it's different. Now there is a very strong hatred for the American leaders. Those leaders have created a program based on fear. They have made everyone frightened, all the time. Once you do that, you can control the public. The Republicans never stop talking about fear and terrorism. I like the old philosophy from FDR: you have nothing to fear but fear itself.

Amelia Ceja

California

Amelia Ceja, the president of Ceja Vineyards, is the first Mexican American woman to be president of a wine production company in North America.

You mentioned something earlier about Democrats liking good food and wine.

I was just having fun; however, wine and food have been a part of my life since I was younger.

Tell me a little about why you are a Democrat?

The party's platform—its philosophy—is closer to mine, which is to govern for the people, by the people, and to give everyone an opportunity to follow his or her dreams. Democrats embrace immigrants, and I am an immigrant. I was born in Mexico, and because of my parents' encouragement, love, and dedication, I went to college. I've been fortunate that my father had the vision to take his family to the United States. He was a migrant farmworker, and we came from a small village in Mexico.

He first came as a migrant worker without the family?

He started coming to the United States in the late 1940s, early 1950s, picking melons, lettuce, tomatoes, in places along the West Coast. It worked out well for me because I could have ended up in Fresno or somewhere else, but it was the Napa Valley he fell in love with. He brought my family here in 1967. I started seventh grade without knowing a word of English, and now I am at the helm of one of the most prestigious small wineries in the Napa Valley. I feel like it is exactly what my father foresaw for his family. I am an immigrant, and now I am going to be pouring my wine at a Margaux event in Bordeaux next month. I began working in the vineyards and now I own them. I am the perfect poster child of the American dream. That's exactly what the Democratic Party stands for.

So, your father brought you here legally then? You were not illegal aliens?

No one is illegal, darling. No human being is illegal. Some people don't have the proper documentation, but that is different. And yes, I came here with a permanent resident visa—a green card. And now I have made a contribution to the wine industry, and I have been paying lots of taxes, so it is symbiotic. Everyone who comes here benefits and so does the country. But it has gotten so difficult to get documents, and agriculture is dependant on the labor force of immigrants. Without the Mexican labor force, there would not be a wine industry, period. The proposed immigration reform upsets me very much because immigrants are criminalized.

When did you first vote?

I became a citizen seventeen years ago, and I'm fortunate to have voted for Bill Clinton—I'd vote for him again.

Had you thought about becoming a citizen before that?

You have to understand that I had a loyalty to the place I came from. But once I made that decision, to become a citizen, I took it very seriously. I disagree with those who say that our vote does not matter. This wonderful country—it's not a perfect democracy, but it's one where I can say how I feel about anything, and I'm not put down. I'm allowed to speak. It's not easy, because it never is, but here it is less difficult.

Which of your wines is the most Democratic?

All of our nine wines that we produce, from our seductive pinot noir, to our crisp chardonnay, to our beautifully balanced Dulce Beso, have all been produced for Democratic reasons. We are bringing wine back to the people and that is a Democratic principle. Wine producers have made wine an elitist beverage, and often there are obstacles to the simple and pure enjoyment of it. I think if you like wine, enjoy it with whatever food you like, and don't allow anyone to dictate what you feel. Wine is the most Democratic of all beverages.

Min Jin Lee

New York and Tokyo, Japan

Min Jin Lee has won numerous fellowships and writing awards, including the William Peden Prize in Fiction from the *Missouri Review* and the *Narrative* Prize for new and emerging writers. Her debut novel, *Free Food for Millionaires*, is a Book Sense #1 Pick, a *New York Times* Editors' Choice and a national best seller.

Tone

In 1992, I was a second-year law student at Georgetown University. I went to my classes and did my assignments competently, but school did not occupy me enough. For good times, I had a boyfriend in New York City, and in an attempt to do some good, I worked as a tutor for the Literacy Volunteers of America. In order to avoid securities law and torts, I read cookbooks. On Saturdays, I baked currant scones and quiches in my white Magic Chef oven—treats alien to my Korean-American background. Still with time to spare and to allay my Presbyterian anxiety of idle hands, I even answered a flier taped to a lunchroom wall.

Consequently, on a school night, I found myself with half a dozen Asian American law students from the D.C. area in a darkened and mostly empty office building in Farragut North. We were there to conduct a phonathon for the 1992 Clinton-Gore campaign.

The volunteer efforts were led by a sharp lawyer of some Asian background—I do not know which—who had graduated from Yale Law School. He was taking a year off from his New York corporate firm life to work for the campaign. He was nice looking in a starchy sort of way, and sufficiently full of beans. I liked him. It was obvious that he was trying to help a bigger cause. If I had known better at the time, I would've been able to see that he was, like me, someone who wouldn't make it always as a lawyer. After a brief overview, he handed out scripts and computer-generated phone lists of people with Asian surnames, and we, the volunteers, were assigned to our respective posts.

They hung up on me. I had been warned of such eventualities. It was, after all, dinnertime for most families. Now, as a thirty-nine-year-old mom of a fourth grader who needs to eat at seven, no doubt, I, too, might have given the younger, earnest me, the brush-off. Then, there were those who answered the phone and did not speak English. I heard Chinese, Korean, Vietnamese, and I want to say Hindi, but I can't be sure. I apologized and moved down the list. Not one person was pleased to be asked: What is your party affiliation? or, Who are you likely to vote for in the November election? The respondent might have answered the phone initially with warmth, but as soon as I reached these questions in my script, I got silence, occasionally hostility, but the tone I had neither expected nor been warned of was fear.

Years later, I took a fiction-writing workshop taught by the wonderful writer Lan Samantha Chang. She said, "Tone is the attitude the narrator has toward the subject."

You can hear tone in writing: irritation, bemusement, generosity, love, anxiety. I find Chang's definition handy in general, because tone is ever present, and it often reveals a person's truer point of view. It is easiest to hear tone in a person's voice.

That night, I was sitting in a borrowed desk in a deserted office, a beige phone propped at my ear, and in my line of sight, a dot matrix Asian surname on a green and white printout. I understood the speaker's neutral words like yes, no, and why, but I heard the speaker's tone—his complicated attitude toward politics and the possibility of two strangers having a safe dialogue. When I grasped this person's fear, I wanted to assure him that I was just an ambivalent law student who possessed, at best, mild political convictions and was game to fliers on cafeteria walls. Americans of all stripes probably have no strong wish to disclose party identities or voting patterns, but as I continued to go down the list, it occurred to me that those who had immigrated from nations with newer democracies or had fled countries held captive by totalitarian leaders might feel far greater reluctance to giving up political affiliations to law students who call at the dinner hour. In 1992 and today, sadly, the public acknowledgment of a vote might lead to adverse socioeconomic repercussions, imprisonment, or possibly death in too many countries to name. I was born in South Korea in 1968— the lower half of a divided peninsula with its own troubled history. Yet, I have been an immigrant since I was seven, and I am a naturalized citizen in a land now so free that I can almost be forgetful of its Exclusion Acts, internment, anti-miscegenation laws, and Jim Crow.

To my mind, Clinton was superior to Bush, but if you had pushed me hard on my leanings at the time, I wouldn't have been able to give you much more than the serviceable answers of a twenty-two-year-old girl who was more concerned about her boyfriend in New York, old Russian novels, and the flakiness of scratch pie crust than the choice of her nation's leaders. Of my fifty or so calls that night, I doubt I was persuasive on behalf of, or much help to, Messrs. Clinton and Gore, but those disembodied voices forced me to think more deeply about democracy and why I was a Democrat. The Democrats liked immigrants, protected the elderly, favored unions, were pro-choice; they supported many social services and public schools of which I'd been a beneficiary. These were my interests, so the Democratic Party was my team. This party made me feel more secure—less afraid for our national future.

I don't know how beneficial phonathons are to political campaigns, but I did learn that it is quite something not to be afraid to make a call, to answer a call, and to say what I am and what I believe in.

Melissa Etheridge

California

Rock musician Melissa Etheridge grew up in Kansas, the daughter of a Republican father and a Democratic mother. Two Grammy Awards and an Oscar are among the many honors she has received. Her tenth album, *The Awakening*, was released in 2007.

How did you end up a Democrat?

When I moved to California, I became involved in the women's movement and the gay movement. I remember a woman who was involved in politics coming up to me with the newspaper and saying, "Look, these are the candidates we are endorsing." I thought, "That's interesting, they're all Democrats." Everyone I knew who was politically aware was a Democrat. They started explaining it all to me, mostly about social issues. And they would ask me to play music at their fundraisers and rallies. It's funny, being the entertainer, you become educated inadvertently. So I started offering my services. In 1988 my first record came out, and as my star started to rise, or whatever, in the industry, I was approached by Alan Hergott, a powerful lawyer in Hollywood. He's also a big political contributor, and he's gay. The gay community in Hollywood is very organized. They were good people. I was seeing the work they did, and I admired it. But I was closeted. I wasn't openly gay—or at least I wasn't telling anybody in the press.

AIDS was the issue that really did it for me. Urvashi Vaid inspired me to be proud about being gay. She's the one who snuck into a speech being given by Bush Senior with a sign that said, "Why haven't you said the word AIDS?" They had to drag her out. That issue brought our community together in a really significant way. We started organizing, we started raising money. It really solidified us. The more I saw friends dying, the more outraged I got. Then when the 1992 race came, when my community got behind Bill Clinton, I did, too. I raised money, I was at rallies, I played, I sang. I felt so great about it that, during the inaugural week, at the gay and lesbian ball I came out publicly as a lesbian.

What does being a Democrat mean to you?

Being a Democrat means knowing to your core what our forefathers intended in creating this great American experience. The great documents of the Constitution and the Bill of Rights. Knowing to your core that it means everyone is endowed by our creator—*everyone*; the creator doesn't make mistakes—every single living being is endowed by our creator with these unalienable rights. Life, liberty, and the pursuit of happiness. The pursuit of happiness. Happiness! It freaks people out because so much of our society is built on commerce, on capitalism. But that's what our forefathers said over two hundred years ago, these crazy men—Thomas Jefferson, Ben Franklin. They would be considered crazy hippies now! The pursuit of happiness. That hope, and that dedication to our country, has found its way solely into the Democrat party.

What do you think of the Log Cabin Republicans?

The most damage is done to the gay community by homophobic gay people. I think Log Cabin Republicans believe in the fundamental Republican platform, or what it used to be anyway—

meaning less government, states' rights, those things that sometimes sound good to me, too. Less tax, that side of it. They are conservative by nature, conservative with their money, but they don't realize that the Republican Party has been taken over by the very fearful. I don't think Karl Rove and George Bush really care if there is man on man, woman on woman. But they hide behind those who are very fearful about it in their religiosity. Fear is their greatest weapon.

When you vote, what do you expect in return?

I expect truthfulness. People make mistakes. Really. But I expect them to listen to the people and be truthful. It's not easy. I know that. We're a whole nation filled with a bunch of different thoughts. Stick to the Constitution, and let's move on.

Seymour Chwast

New York

Seymour Chwast is a founding partner of the celebrated Push Pin Studios, whose distinct style has had a worldwide influence on contemporary visual communications. His designs and illustrations have been used in advertising, animated films, corporate and environmental graphics, books, magazines, posters, packaging, and record covers.

The Good Business Party

Democrats are pragmatic. They want to get ahead, but not at the expense of everyone around them. They realize that a society in which their fellow Americans are also doing well is the best of all possible worlds. So, they look at the records of candidates and administrations and ask themselves: Who's working for the worker? Whose policies create a positive outcome for the most people, for the greater good of the country and the world? Who cares about economic justice for all? Whose programs work best to create a sustainable economy, encourage business growth, protect workers? As Republican icon Bill O'Reilly asks, "Who's really looking out for *you?*"

Lisa Eue Kaliszewski

Minnesota

Lisa Kaliszewski, who grew up in St. Paul, is a waitress at Mickey's Diner in downtown St. Paul, a restaurant listed on the National Register of Historic Places.

Have you been working at Mickey's for a long time?

Just a couple of years, but I've been a waitress for twenty-five years.

So why are you a Democrat?

I'm not really much into politics, but if I had to say, I guess it's because the Democrats are more for people like me.

And how would you describe people like you?

Minimum wage. I'm actually below minimum wage.

Do people talk politics at the counter?

Oh, yeah. There's one guy, I tell him he should run for something.

Do you take part in the discussions?

If it's about something specific, that I'm interested in, I might. Like Social Security. I'm afraid by the time it's my turn, there'll be nothing left.

Let's talk eggs. How do you think Republicans take their eggs?
Probably hard boiled.

Democrats?
Easier. Quicker and easier.

Bernard Rapoport

Texas

Bernard Rapoport is founding chairman and CEO of the
American Income Life Insurance Company in Waco, Texas.
Included among America's forty most generous philanthropists
by *Fortune* magazine, he is chairman of the Bernard and Audre
Rapoport Foundation, which supports education, social justice,
and liberal political causes

Was your father a Democrat?

No, Papa was a Marxist when he came to the United States from
Russia in 1913, and then when Stalin came in, he realized Stalin
wasn't a Marxist, he was a dictator, so consequently, he became a
Socialist.

When did you realize that you were a Democrat?

I was always a Democrat. Now, socialism is not something that
frightens me as it does a lot of people because I think the concept
of socialism is wonderful. But capitalism is the only workable system. The problem is we don't have capitalism anymore; we have
monopolies. Essentially what we have in our society is, we have
one percent—and I am in that one percent—that has more assets

then the bottom one hundred million Americans. How is that a sustainable society?

Is there one ideal that means "Democrat" to you?

I think that when we use the word "opportunity," we mean it for all Americans. I came out of a very poor home, but I never felt poor because I had a father who felt education was the most important thing. And I used that education.

You mentioned FDR and some of the programs he instituted, and how he wanted more equitable distribution of wealth. How would you go about trying to accomplish the same thing now?

The first thing they should do is increase taxes on the rich. You can't do anything without money, and we have all these tax avoidance schemes for people with money to escape taxes, legal ways. And I'm one who takes advantage of them, too! They didn't put any angelic blood in me. I always tell everyone that I want a fairer society because you can not trust me, either. 'Cause when I run a business, I'm a predator. I want to make the most money I can. I want rules that would limit me in some of the things that I was able to do so that we can have a better society.

Anything else?

You have a hundred million who don't have very much. If we had a living minimum wage—say ten or eleven dollars an hour—that bottom hundred million would have more money, and what would they do? They'd spend it. Big business today is myopic. The reality is that businesses would make more money if they had enough foresight to understand what the bottom hundred million people could do if we had the good sense to insure them a good life.

With certain people I'm talking to, I'm noticing frustration with the Party. What do you think has kept you proud to be a Democrat?

In life, you make choices. Between Republicans and Democrats, I take the Democrats. If we still had a Socialist Party, I would be helpful to it. I would still be a Democrat, but I would be helpful to it because I think we need the pressure that a socialist philosophy permeates throughout our society.

When I was a kid, we lived all over the Midwest, and my mother's favorite place was Milwaukee because the mayor was a Socialist. She thought his programs were terrific.

I was raised in Texas, but I want to tell you something: the two greatest states in this country are Minnesota and Wisconsin. Wisconsin had the La Follettes [the family whose members were leaders of the Midwest Progressive movement], who laid a foundation, the remnants of which are still there. And Minnesota had the Farm and Labor Party. Those states are the two cleanest states in the United States. In Texas, we got a scandal every fifteen minutes.

Jack Geiger

Kansas

Jack Geiger is a sixth-generation Kansas farmer in Robinson, Kansas.
Two of his brothers are also farmers—and fellow Democrats.

What do you raise on your farm?

We're a diversified farm. We raise a lot of small grains. Wheat and clover. Also, cattle.

How large is the farm?

Sizable—probably over five hundred acres.

Why are you a Democrat?

Philosophical reasons. I was raised that way and I believe that way. All of my education and all of my life experience has indicated to me that I made the correct choice. I have never doubted that I should be a Democrat.

What do you think about the idea that all farmers are Republicans?

Farmers *are* Republican, but I'm a certified organic farmer.

But you're still a farmer?

Yeah, but most conventional farmers are Republicans.

Was it always that way?

No, in Kansas here, with the older generation, you had more Democrats.

Why do you think it shifted to be more Republican?

A lot of people got mad at Jimmy Carter for the grain embargo. People are funny. They'll get one impression and stick with it even when they know it's wrong or no longer relevant. People are creatures of habit.

Is there one issue or ideal that means "Democrat" to you?

I think that the Democrats as a general rule work for economic justice and believe in economic justice. That is why I'm a Democrat.

Who do you think symbolizes the Democrats?

I think Jimmy Carter typifies Democrat. I own all of his books. He was a farmer, and he's humble, and he is very determined to work for justice and peace. Other ex-presidents are playing golf, but Jimmy Carter is still working. He is one of my heroes. I'm not mad at the grain embargo and the fallout from that. He didn't bring on the rural depression. A lot of farmers blame him for the farm crisis of the early 1980s. From what I've studied, that was one of those deals where the next president gets blamed for an economic downturn he didn't create.

What do you expect in return for your vote?

Honesty. That's all I want out of any politician. To be honest with you, I'm an elected Democrat myself. Township trustee for Robinson Township.

Frank E. Olivieri

New Jersey

Frank E. Olivieri is the owner of Pat's King of Steaks in Philadelphia.
His grandfather, Harry Olivieri, and Harry's brother Pat, along
with their employee Joe Lorenzo, are credited with inventing
the Philly cheesesteak.

How long have you been in the cheesesteak business?

I'm forty-three, and I'm working here since I was eleven. My family started the business in 1930.

So why are you a Democrat?

I am a Democrat because it's the lesser of the two evils, without being sarcastic. Although I do think the Democrats represent more of the common people. The Republicans are more representative of big business, which gets the big tax breaks. The middle class—right now they are the people who are supporting and running the county and bearing the tax burden. The Democrats represent people like myself.

What do you expect for your vote?

I expect some level of honesty in return, and I expect a hundred percent representation of my opinion and that of the other people in the party. That may be like believing in Santa or the Tooth Fairy, but still . . .

Do you live in Philly?

No, I used to, but in 1987 I moved to the Communist state of New Jersey.

Why Communist?

Your Second Amendment rights are not recognized in New Jersey! The gun control laws are too stiff! I'm a firm believer in regulating it, but not to the point where you can't own or carry. When I lived in Pennsylvania, I had a permit to carry—twenty-four hours—a concealed weapon. I didn't abuse the privilege, but I'm a business owner, and I felt I needed it. The ones who have the guns illegally are the ones committing the crimes.

Are you a hunter as well?

No, I don't believe in killing animals. Except cows.

How do Democrats take their cheesesteaks?

With Cheese Whiz and fried onions—the classic way. That's the way I'd take it if I were marooned on a desert island, but the only island I'm ever on is where I summer, in Brigantine, New Jersey, and it's heavily Republican. I've been summering there since 1972. I've been asked to run for office. My friends there are all Republicans. But I say, "Sorry, guys, if I ran, it would have to be as a Democrat."

Sheila McGee

Kentucky

For seventeen years, Sheila McGee has worked in Louisville
at Lear Corporation, which makes seats for Ford automobiles.
She chairs the women's committee of Local 43 of the United
Auto Workers.

One big issue for us at the plant is the outsourcing of jobs. The
Republicans really allow that to happen when they're in charge.
Here in Kentucky, a Republican swipe of the pen took away our organized bargaining. The union got the right to collective bargaining a long time ago; then Governor Fletcher, who's a Republican,
came in a few years ago, and just like that, he took it away. We're
going through contracts right now. And their threat is, if we don't
do what they say, they're going to outsource the job. They're taking away a lot of our health benefits, too. It used to be free; all you
had to do was pay for the co-pay, ten dollars, and prescriptions
were five dollars. Now we've got to pay per family, thirty-two dollars per person. It doesn't matter how many you've got; it's thirty-
two dollars a person per week.

I have always been a Democrat, though I didn't pay close attention to politics until my first marriage. My ex-husband's family
was very political here in Louisville. The reason I'm a Democrat

is that, over the years, I followed the voting records of officials to see if they were for working people, Middle America. I looked at the records and asked myself, would it do me any good voting for a Republican or Democrat? The Republicans didn't do me any good, but the Democrats, definitely. They're for the working family. They're for trying to get the minimum wage back up, for keeping the gas prices down. It seems like the Republicans are out for themselves. They're just out for filling their pockets and doing their dirt. They'll lie to you in your face. They always start off with, "We're going to do this for schools, we're going to do this for the working family, we're going to take care of the roads," or whatever, and they don't follow through on anything. The Democrats are more reliable. I mean, not all Democrats are fair. I'm sure they've got a quota to fill, too, of bad Democrats. But the stuff they do is minor compared to Republicans. Look at the world now and the way it was with Bill Clinton. He did some good things. Even though he went through a bad fall there, he did some good things. I didn't see the world falling apart the way it is right now with gas prices, and fighting over nuclear war, and war in Iraq and Iran and all that. I mean, he didn't make the world fall apart like that. He had one little flaw.

I have three grown children, and one fifteen-year-old still at home, and ten grandchildren. They're stuck with me whether they like it or not, so Democrat is what they hear!

Andrew Tobias

Florida and New York

Andrew Tobias is the author of *The Only Investment Guide You'll Ever Need*, which has sold more than a million copies, and *The Best Little Boy in the World*, which was added to the Modern Library series to mark the twenty-fifth anniversary of its original, pseudonymous publication. His *Managing Your Money* was an early software best seller.

Net Worth Is Nice, But Self Worth Is Even Nicer

Imagine my surprise—I am treasurer of the Democratic National Committee (DNC)—when I got in the mail a certificate from my counterpart, the treasurer of the *Republican* National Committee (RNC), in recognition of my "proven commitment and dedication to the Republican Party." It came along with a four-page fundraising letter and was suitable for framing.

Direct mail inanities can befall anyone, and perhaps I should take this opportunity to apologize for anything inane you may have gotten from *us*. I mention my RNC certificate simply as proof that I am not one of those people who would never, ever vote for a Republican. Having once or twice in the past sent checks to Republicans (I was young! I was foolish!) I have ever since gotten warm personal letters from the most remarkable people. Newt Gingrich was writing me for a while. The chairman of Christian Voice has written me more than once to warn me—in the most strident terms—against . . . well, people like me.

Anyway, my point is that I don't consider myself a mindless partisan, even though I grew up in a Democratic household. And I don't agree with everything Democrats have ever done, although I think our intentions were usually good. But what I think has happened is that the whole political landscape has shifted dramatically to the right.

Our party certainly still has its extreme liberals—and God bless 'em. But by and large, we have moved to the center.

The leadership of the other party, by contrast, has moved so far right it's almost fallen over the edge.

So my pitch to my Republican friends—some of whom have even given me nice big checks for the Democratic Party—is, "Help us help you get your party back."

The irony is that on the one bedrock Republican issue—fiscal prudence—the Republican leadership has totally lost its mind. The national debt, accumulated since 1776, will be around $10 trillion by the time Bush leaves office. Of this, nearly $8 trillion— 80 percent!—will have been racked up under just three presidents: Reagan, Bush, and Bush. The debt has grown so large under Republican stewardship that just the *interest* consumes 40 percent of all the money we Americans pay in personal income tax each year.

Worse still, all this debt has been piled up not to build world-leading infrastructure or world-beating educational success; but rather, in large part, to grant massive tax cuts to the rich.

I don't think it's fair. And I don't want to live in a country where, ultimately, the top 2 percent will be guarded from everyone else by sentries with machine guns.

Amazingly, we Democrats have become the party of fiscal responsibility.

Not every last congressman and senator is on the same page. But most are. The Clinton-Gore administration made a very clear choice for fiscal prudence right from the start, turning deficits to surplus. As soon as the Republicans regained control, it was back to tax cuts for "billionheirs" and a huge expansion in "earmarks," never mind the debt.

The fact is, the stock market historically does better under Democrats than Republicans. The economy historically does better under Democrats than Republicans. My net worth—and yours—is likely to do better under Democrats than Republicans.

What Democrats get, I think, perhaps more than the other party's leadership—which fights so hard against any increase in the minimum wage and bashes with such relish our foreign aid to poorer nations—is this: that in an increasingly interdependent world, if "they" do better, we do better, too.

If "they" do better, we do better, too.

It is a message of inclusion, of fairness, of opportunity, and of community.

If "they" do better, we do better, too.

Certainly if you're in "the bottom 99 percent," but even, I think, over the long run, if you're rich, Democrats are better for your net worth.

But forget all that. Assume, if you want, that your family will be just as prosperous and secure, your net worth just as robust, under either party. That's a lot to assume, if you ask me, but go ahead.

What good is net worth without self worth?

Appreciation of your stock portfolio without, also, a sense that you are appreciated as a person?

And this is where, to me, the Democrats truly shine.

The Democratic Party has said time and again, in words and actions, that "America doesn't have a person to waste."

The Democratic Party welcomes and celebrates diversity.

The thirteen Republican House managers walk into the room for their 1998 impeachment proceeding and you've got . . . thirteen white guys. The ten 2008 Republican presidential candidates walk onto the stage and you've got . . . ten white guys.

This is not to knock white guys. My boyfriend's a white guy. But in 2008, America is more than that, and we are the richer for it.

When I was just starting out as DNC treasurer, Joe Andrew was party chair. Asked to say a few words at an event we attended together, he said something so completely unscripted and natural and from the heart, that I have been quoting it ever since. "You know," he said, *"we're Democrats.* We don't care whether you're black or you're white or you're green or you're purple. We don't care whether you walked in here or you *rolled* in here. We don't care what religion you are or what gender you are or what gender you hold hands with—so long as you hold hands. You are welcome in the Democratic Party."

And that's the deal. *So long as you hold hands.* We are one magnificently diverse country. Opportunity for all; special privilege for none; a community that encourages the best in all of us. The Democrats really mean it.

★5★

The Party
of Former Independents

Given the diversity and size of the country's population, it is odd, indeed, that no third or fourth or fifth political party has ever taken significant root in the United States. From the Socialists to the Libertarians to the Greens, many have attempted to make inroads into the political process, with varying levels of success. Young voters, supportive of democratic principles but eager to make their own way politically, often are drawn to Independent movements. Many ultimately register with the Democratic Party, however, after realizing that within its ranks it is possible to be both free thinking and politically productive. The strongest Independent efforts have served primarily to prove the "spoiler" theory: Independents may help determine the outcome of an election, but not in favor of their own candidates. The 2000 election was the most striking example of the power of Independents. As a result of this, and for a variety of other reasons, a number of diehard Independents have registered, or re-registered, as Democrats.

Frank McCourt

New York and Connecticut

Frank McCourt was born in Brooklyn and grew up in Ireland.
For thirty years he taught in New York City high schools. His
first book, *Angela's Ashes*, won the Pulitzer Prize, the National
Book Critics Circle Award, and the Los Angeles Times Book
Award. His most recent book is *Angela and the Baby Jesus*.

*So, you were a Democrat, and you became an Independent, and now
you're going to switch back? What happened?*

I keep saying to my poor wife, Ellen, that I'm always waiting to
hear a voice, and I haven't heard any voices lately. Even though
I admired Clinton, he still wasn't the voice. I wanted him to rise
above it, but he was pulled down by his genitalia. I didn't blame
him. I just thought it was disgusting the way they went after him.
I expect the Republicans to be wary and look over their shoulders
and not to offend the corporation, but I always looked on the
Democrats as the people with vision and commitment and conviction and passion, and I wasn't hearing it. So out of pure ire, I
registered as an Independent. I forgot about it, then I went to vote
as a Democrat up in Connecticut and they reminded me. So I will
be back again on the Democratic rolls.

So why are you—were you and are you—a Democrat?

It's genetic. Growing up in Ireland we were always told that nothing in America would have happened without the Irish. We built everything. The White House, the Empire State Building, the Brooklyn Bridge. The Republicans were country club people, they were Protestants. That's how we viewed them. I read the labor history—what the Irish did in America—and it was all Democratic. Tammany Hall [New York's legendary Democratic political machine]. I was always fascinated with Tammany Hall, even though they were as corrupt as an old ulcer. They were the ones that gave the poor the turkey at Christmas, and the means to cook it. Someone said, the Republicans gave a turkey, too, but they forget you have to have a way of cooking it. The Democrats would think of that. So, it was the Irish thing, the Catholic thing, the genetic thing, the historical thing, and then you engage in that serious activity called thinking for yourself, and some of us Irish are not equipped for that independent thinking. That's alright. I like the idea of the organization. It's great to be a radical, but you ought to be a radical within your own group, which is what I am, in a way. I am always reminded of an Irish politician named Conor Cruise O'Brien, who used to be in the U.N. here. He belonged to the Labour Party in Ireland. He said, "I belong to the Labour Party because I think they are kinder." That's what it boils down to. I think the Democrats are kinder than the Republicans. For me, that's the umbrella virtue.

Is there one issue or ideal that means "Democrat" to you?

My business most of my life was education, and I think they are somewhat more committed to public education than the other party. Now don't pin me down on that. I think they are, though they've fallen into step behind that law, No Child Left Behind.

Teddy Kennedy is the main man in education in the Senate, and he's in lockstep with the Bush crowd in the matter of No Child Left Behind.

What don't you like about No Child Left Behind?
Testing, testing, testing. You think: how did this country become so great before they started testing the life out of these kids?

When was the first time you voted?
I voted for Adlai Stevenson. I was in Germany in the army. It was Adlai Stevenson in 1952 and '56, and then that glorious moment for John Kennedy in '60 and ever since I've always voted Democratic. I mean, I couldn't vote for a Republican. Not yet.

Did you think of Adlai Stevenson as a Democrat, or as a candidate?
I thought about him as a Democrat because I have a distinct revulsion toward the Republican Party.

Do you have any Republican friends?
I have some who recently have become somewhat right-wing. It's hard for me, especially in the matter of the war. It raised my ire. Because they can't see.

Are they still supporting the war?
Yes. Well, they're waffling a bit now. This is the thing that pisses me off—that you have to belong to one thing or another. Generally, I think Democratic and I always vote Democratic. But I like to look at what is going on and pause a moment with some skepticism. I think that is the greatest gift you can have in the face of politics.

Lyndon Wong

California

Lyndon Wong is a software marketer and technologist at Yahoo!.
He has worked previously at ExciteAtHome, Accenture, and several other venture-backed startups in Silicon Valley.

Have you always been a Democrat?

No. Currently I'm a registered Democrat, but I have registered Independent in the past. I have always had friends across the political spectrum and respected their various views.

What attracted you to the Democrats?

Probably the recognition of a centrist position, combining a thoughtfully progressive outlook with a grounded view on fiscal matters. Also, Jimmy Carter. Particularly since leaving the White House, Carter encapsulates much of what has drawn me to the Democrats of my lifetime: compassion, thoughtfulness, idealism. The Democrats as a whole share a forward-thinking temper. We tend to strive to be "of our time." I identify with that outlook.

Can you think of any experience or incident that validated your decision to be a Democrat?

A collection of individuals and events support my decision to be a Democrat. I include in that collection Gavin Newsom's attempt as mayor of San Francisco to legally recognize same-sex marriages.

Is there one issue that is more important to you than any other?

I struggle to highlight one single issue above the rest. Well, maybe minimizing our carbon footprint—I hope that's not just an issue for Democrats.

Is there anything you don't like about the Democrats?

Irrational exuberance with social programs. Perhaps that comes inevitably with idealism.

Is there any piece of art that says "Democrat" to you?

In my mind, most art and architecture deemed modern in its time captures the spirit of Democrats, or more accurately, progressives. The opposite sentiment, a conservative outlook, seems to favor the traditional in architecture and the arts. It takes a progressive spirit to embrace something without obvious precedent. By this measure, Bill Clinton's Presidential Library fits—how convenient for this theory that he's also a Democrat ;-). Perhaps an even better example is the Sea Ranch community in California, which after forty years still freshly embodies a forward-looking outlook on life and our relationship to the natural environment.

Norman Solomon

California

Norman Solomon is a syndicated columnist, author, and
activist. His latest books are *War Made Easy: How Presidents
and Pundits Keep Spinning Us to Death* and *Made Love, Got War:
Close Encounters with America's Warfare State.*

Why am I a Democrat? In a word: Republicans.

Of course it's not that simple. Being the "lesser of two evils"
is not a term of endearment or a solid basis for support. But the
best reason for being a Democrat in 2008, and well beyond, is the
extreme and dangerous agenda of the Republican Party. My own
desires for a third-party effort have given way to a reluctant belief
that—like it or not, and I often don't—the path to progressive
political change runs through the Democratic Party. History has
shown us that no other political party has the capacity to block
the GOP. At times in past decades, I'd had hope that a third-party
challenge from the left could pull the Democratic Party away from
the deadly "center" of corporatism, high military spending, and
war. In 1980, the Barry Commoner presidential campaign (under
the banner of the Citizens Party) drew my interest and my vote.
Commoner had scant impact on the election, which ushered in
the era of Ronald Reagan, and with it, deregulation, attacks on
the public sector, and an escalating military budget (trends that

had begun during the last two years of the Carter presidency). I was gloomy at Reagan's initial victory, and re-election, but I clung to the idea that the most important thing—no matter who sat in the Oval Office—would be activism at the grassroots.

But it's enormously important who runs the Executive Branch, wields a majority in Congress, and selects judges throughout the federal judiciary. Overall, dreadful as Democratic administrations have often been, Republican administrations have been appreciably worse.

Before the 2000 election, I was one of many progressive voters who was disappointed with the Clinton-Gore administration. From poverty to trade to environmental protection to Pentagon budgets, their policies showed them to be Republican Lite. And so I joined the Nader camp, ready to respond to Clinton-Gore with an electoral kick in the pants. The consequences of a George W. Bush administration at that point were abstract. We learned too late how miscalculated the Nader movement was.

By the time 2004 came around, I not only wanted nothing to do with Nader's new presidential campaign—I actively worked against it, urging a vote for the Kerry-Edwards ticket in all "non-safe-states" where the electoral votes were up for grabs.

The Democratic congressional majority that took office in early 2007 turned out to be cowardly and accommodating to the GOP agenda in many respects. Yet our best response is to actively support more progressive candidates in Democratic primaries. Efforts to throw a scare into the Democrats by costing them elections with third-party "spoiler" campaigns have proved to be both ineffective and counterproductive for progressive goals. What *does* hold out real promise is painstaking work inside and outside the Democratic Party—running candidates in the primaries while also organizing grassroots movements outside the party. That's why I support Progressive Democrats of America, a national group with an inside/outside strategy that aims "to build a party and government controlled by citizens, not corporate elites—with policies that serve the broad public interest, not just private interests."

Often, for understandable reasons, people on the left make sweeping denunciations of "the Democrats." But in Congress and other public offices, there are Democrats and Democrats. Our tasks include replacing the party's Blue Dogs with genuine progressives. It won't be easy. But we should never have believed anyone who promised us a rose garden.

Amanda Palmer

Massachusetts

Along with being one half of the acclaimed punk cabaret duo,
The Dresden Dolls, pianist and vocalist Amanda Palmer performs
and records as a solo artist. *Who Killed Amanda Palmer* is her first
solo LP.

*How do you find the politics in the music business? It seems to be mostly
Democrats, no?*

Sure, but you're talking to a musician in a punk cabaret band! Try
hanging out with the musicians who play in cover bands in bars in
Alabama. Different story.

*True, although maybe there's a Republican punk cabaret band somewhere.
Does Ted Nugent qualify?*

Music is as diverse as anything else. Travel around and you'll find
a lot of Republican rock bands and a lot of Christian rock bands,
and a lot of anarchic rock bands. Certainly it is often hard for me
to understand why people with a commitment and a passion for
art don't share my political views, but that's just me.

Is there any song, yours or anyone else's, that says "Democrat" to you?

The band is pretty well-known for a cover we do of Black Sabbath's "War Pigs." We were pulling that out pretty frequently during the last election. There's that great lyric about politicians starting wars, but leaving the actual fighting to the poor.

Where are you from originally?

I grew up in Lexington, Massachusetts—the birthplace of American liberty.

Were your parents involved in politics at all?

Very much so, mostly local politics. My stepfather was on the school committee and the town meeting for a long time. And when he retired, my stepfather traveled and campaigned a bit for John Kerry. The town I grew up in is really Democratic.

What's your personal political history?

I've never been overtly political unless you count the summer when I was fourteen and a budding Libertarian and I campaigned for Lenora Fulani. I have switched my registration back and forth between Independent and Democrat, but I've been predominantly Democrat since I was in high school. I was actually banned from social studies class for wearing a shirt that said "Lick Bush in '88," which I thought was hilarious.

What made you switch back and forth?

Like many people of my generation—I'm thirty-one—I got confused in my twenties by what "Democrat" was supposed to stand for. It seemed like some kind of wishy-washy middle ground. If you look at the definitions of what it means to be a Democrat and what it means to be a Republican, there is the theoretical, and then there's the practical, and they don't always line up. When I started looking at what these people actually *do*, I decided to search elsewhere. I got a taste of what the Libertarians were doing, and some of that sounded right. I took at look at the Green Rainbow Party, and much of that seemed right. And then there was my high school Ayn Rand phase, when I thought, "Oh, my God, I think I'm a Republican! Smart people might just be better than dumb people!"

What do you mean by the wishy-washy middle ground?

One thing that is frightening, as politics has become so confusing and convoluted, is that a lot of people of my generation have just turned their backs and said, "I can't make any sense of this, so why should I vote?" My band, The Dresden Dolls, we were working in partnership with Music for America, which is a generally nonpartisan organization that registers people to vote at rock shows. They were working really aggressively during the last election, which was when we were on tour, so they were at our shows. This feeling of "why bother" was coming up a lot in discussions. You heard a lot of people saying, "I really don't think it's going to make any difference."

Probably in part because they were at an impressionable age during the 2000 election.

Right. To see what happened with that election—it was a massive blow to the psyche of so many people.

What do you except from the Democrats in return for your vote?

I like to think that people will stand by a position and not flip-flop around. That's one thing that keeps people of my generation from

getting involved in politics, or even voting: seeing a lot of waffling politicians and then just throwing our hands in the air. The
problem is that politicians rarely seem like people. They seem like
actors. Very shiftable. For someone to really stake a goal in the
ground—a position—and see it through is what I would expect.

You mentioned your stepfather earlier. Was your mother political, also?

They both encouraged me to vote and to think for myself. My
mom often bought me to the polls with her when I was a kid. I
would wait outside while she voted. I was thinking what a great
thing that is to do with your kids. You'd be amazed at the number
of people who don't know what is involved. They've never voted.
It's like—let's say you'd never been to the dentist before, and
you're terrified, and you don't even know where to start. If you
bring your kids with you, they understand that voting is part of
everyday life. You go to the grocery store, you go to the bank, and,
every once in a while, you go to vote.

Random Thoughts on Democrats

by Democrats and One Republican

I don't belong to any organized political faith. I am a Democrat.

Will Rogers while introducing California Governor James Rolph
at an event in San Francisco in 1930

Philosophy? I am a Christian and a Democrat—that's all.

Franklin D. Roosevelt to a young reporter quizzing him on his beliefs,
as recalled by Labor Secretary Frances Perkins in her 1946 book,
The Roosevelt I Knew

In this world of sin and sorrow there is always something to be
thankful for. As for me, I rejoice that I am not a Republican.

H. L. Mencken among the epigrams he included in *A Mencken
Chrestomathy* (1949)

If [the Republicans] will stop telling lies about the Democrats,
we will stop telling the truth about them.

Adlai Stevenson during the 1952 presidential campaign

Nixon in the last seven days has called me an economic
ignoramus, a Pied Piper, and all the rest. I just confine myself
to calling him a Republican. But he says that is really getting low.

John F. Kennedy from a speech given in the Bronx, New York, during
the 1960 presidential campaign

I sent my flowers across the hall to Mrs. Nixon but her husband
remembered what a Democrat I am and sent them back.

Bette Davis reminiscing about a political encounter during a 1987
interview with Joan Rivers

. . . because it is easier to give someone the finger than a helping
hand.

Mike Royko on why it is harder to be a liberal than a conservative,
from a 1995 *Chicago Tribune* column

Though it is sometimes difficult and painful to say, I am pleased
I live in a world with Republicans, if only to set in spectacular
relief the overwhelming good sense of [the Democratic] Party.

Ken Burns while introducing Al Gore at an event in New Hampshire
in 1998

As people do better, they start voting like Republicans—unless
they have too much education and vote Democratic, which
proves there can be too much of a good thing.

Karl Rove in a 2001 *New Yorker* interview

When I got out of the military, I looked at both parties. I'm
pro-choice, pro-affirmative action, pro-environment, pro-labor.
I was either going to be the loneliest Republican in America
or I was going to be a happy Democrat.

General Wesley Clark during a Democratic presidential debate in
New Hampshire in 2004

If you want to live like a Republican, you better vote for the Democrats!

Richard Gephardt from his 2004 presidential campaign
stump speech

This is Democratic bedrock: we don't let people lie in the ditch and drive past and pretend not to see them dying. Here on the frozen tundra of Minnesota, if your neighbor's car won't start, you put on your parka and get the jumper cables out and deliver the Sacred Spark that starts their car. Everybody knows this. The logical extension of this spirit is social welfare and the myriad government programs with long dry names all very uninteresting to you until you suddenly need one and then you turn into a Democrat. A liberal is a conservative who's been through treatment.

Garrison Keillor from his 2004 book, *Homegrown Democrat: A Few Plain Thoughts from the Heart of America*

Regrettably, President Reagan made the denial of compassion for the people who needed it most sound like a virtue.

Mario Cuomo to the *New York Times* in the wake of Ronald Reagan's death in 2004

It's innate in me to be a Democrat—a true Southern populist kind of Democrat. There's not a lot of those anymore. I'm not saying I'm right or wrong. That's just the way I feel.

Tim McGraw in a 2006 *Time* magazine interview

I started thinking more after I got out of school.

Warren Buffett when Hillary Clinton asked him, "Why are you a Democrat?" at a fundraising event in California in 2007. The billionaire investor said that he had been president of his college Republican club.

★7★

The Family Party

Given the number of contributors to this book who come from families in which politics was rarely discussed, it is clear that political affiliation is not necessarily inherited. And yet, people who grow up in households devoted to democratic ideals and the party that exemplifies them, and who reach adulthood in agreement with those ideals, tend to stick to the Democratic Party with enthusiasm. Their adherence to the principles at the foundation of the Party is not blind. They went out into the world armed with the lessons they learned at home and found no need to change their allegiance.

Teri Hein

Washington

Teri Hein taught for twenty years at a school for patients and family members of patients at the Fred Hutchinson Cancer Center. She is the founding director of 826 Seattle, a nonprofit writing center for young people, and the author of *Atomic Farmgirl*, a memoir of growing up downwind of the Hanford Nuclear Reservation.

In 1984 my father was an anomaly in our Eastern Washington farming community: a progressive liberal Democrat. Our town, Fairfield, had a population of 350 people, 90 percent of those people living directly or indirectly from the planting and harvesting of the wheat, peas, and lentils that flourished in the Palouse region. Our family didn't actually live in town but rather ten miles out on our farm, although Dad drove daily to Fairfield, especially during harvest season when wheat or peas or lentils were delivered to the silos next to the railroad tracks.

Many of the area's residents had been there for several generations. Most of them were good people. They made casseroles when someone was sick and added a little extra to the offertory on Sundays when there was a special collection for orphans in Africa. Men readily joined the Service Club and women the Ladies' Aide to lend their talents to making our small town the best place it could possibly be. And the majority of them voted Republican.

My father could not understand the fears of undue government intervention that plagued his fellow farmers and made them believe the Republican Party was the right choice. It didn't make sense to him. How could you wave the American flag, but not trust the government, the bedrock of that cloth symbol? It wasn't that he was a fool. Of course he knew about the innate selfishness and corrupt tendencies of anyone with power. But he was determined to be optimistic and to remain convinced that if we were visited, as we are occasionally, by corrupt politicians, they would be voted out or removed from office.

It wasn't that he was more compassionate than his fellow farmers. He just didn't understand how we could feed the poor, care for the mentally ill, provide good education and health care for all, and create a world of equality if the government did not tax us enough to pay for these services and then provide them. He was practical enough to realize that people are just plain too selfish to fully assume responsibility for their fellow humans. People gave money in church but not until it hurt. That's where he perceived the government coming in and using our tax dollars to pay for the things that would make all of our lives better. Wouldn't it be better for all of us, and more economically responsible, to keep people out of prisons and hospitals by providing them with the services that might deter them from ending up in such dire straits? The Republican mantra—that big business trickle-down eventually creates enough jobs to raise the standard of living for all—seemed to him quixotic at best.

My mother couldn't have agreed more, and the two of them instilled fidelity for the Democratic Party in their four daughters.

In 1984, after college and a move to Seattle, I arrived home with a present for my father—a Jesse Jackson for President T-shirt to match the one I'd purchased for myself. Because I was young and naïve I was certain Jackson would win, so profoundly was he able to expound upon the values our family held so strongly. I imagine my father was more pragmatic. Jesse Jackson was a black man running for president in 1984. His greater knowledge did not stop Dad from wearing the T-shirt into Fairfield on trips to the Grain Growers and the John Deere store. Dad never would have actively campaigned for Jesse—he wasn't the campaigning type—but wearing that T-shirt through the streets of Fairfield spoke volumes.

I am a Democrat, in part, because my father would wear that T-shirt. A person must be optimistic that unlikely things can happen in the name of good. My dad instilled in me a belief that we must take care of each other—and the "we" in part is our elected government. While the Democratic Party has not bowled me over lately with its abilities to solve the biggest problems facing us right now, I hold out much more hope that they, not the Republicans, will pick up the mantle of protecting us from ourselves.

My father died last November. His Jesse Jackson T-shirt was long ago worn to shreds and tossed, clearly part of his wardrobe long after Jesse was out of the campaign. I found my Jesse Jackson T-shirt in a box recently, still in relatively good condition. I plan to wear it on Election Day 2008 to salute my father and to demonstrate optimism for a more compassionate future in our United States.

Barbara Janusiak

Wisconsin

Barbara Janusiak has been a registered nurse for thirty years. She works at St. Francis Hospital in Milwaukee and is a member of the Wisconsin Federation of Nurses and Health Professionals.

In my family, there were some very strong Democratic principles, mostly involving looking at what the needs of the community or the world are rather than your individual personal needs. My parents are both Democrats. I grew into being a Democrat from that base. That's true for almost all of us. I have eleven brothers and sisters, and I have one brother who is a Republican. We don't know how it happened.

My dad was a plant manager for a company in Kenosha that made sanitary pipe fittings. He started out as a sweeper, and moved up to become plant manager. He went to high school for only three years, and was self-taught. He can speak Polish, and a little Russian. The union never organized at his plant until after he was in management, but he encouraged his employees to organize, and he was so supportive of me when we were organizing the nurses' union. If I needed to sound off something from a management perspective, I could call him.

I work at the only unionized private hospital in Milwaukee. There has been a move to unionize some of the others. It hasn't happened yet, though many of the nurses want it to. I can kind of tell the Republican and the Democratic doctors. The Republican doctors were so glad to see a Republican president because their personal finances improved. They seem to be the same ones who fear the union.

In an email from one of my friends, I came across a quote from Dwight D. Eisenhower in a letter he wrote to his brother Edgar in 1954. He said, "Should any political party attempt to abolish Social Security, unemployment insurance, and eliminate labor laws and farm programs, you would not hear of that party again in our political history. There is a tiny splinter group, of course, that believes that you can do these things. Among them are a few Texas oil millionaires and an occasional politician or business-man from other areas. Their numbers are negligible, and they are stupid." Isn't that great?

Hector "Tico" Betancourt
Florida

Trained as an engineer, Hector Betancourt worked in the airline
industry before starting a company to sell commercial aircraft and
engine parts. Since selling that company, he has worked in Miami
as an investor in real estate and other ventures.

I am a Democrat, in part, because of my populist views, which
were also the views of my father and grandfather. I have always
seen the Democratic Party as representative of a broad sector of
the population, not favoring one group over another. Also I was
raised Catholic. My Christian beliefs influenced my politics, not
so much ideologically, like some Christians today, but because
Christians believe in the equality of man and the need to measure your fellow man independently of wealth and background.
Christian ideals are somewhat socialistic, in the sense that the
poor are given their place as God's people as much as anyone
else.

My father always instilled in us the view that the more extreme
the members of a society live in terms of their wealth and privilege,
the bigger the chance for revolution. A majority of the have-nots
will become empowered in such a way that they will take whatever steps are necessary to obtain some measure of respectability

and wealth. That's the way it has happened in many other countries, and that is what scares me about our society right now—the gap between the haves and have-nots. To be the richest county in the world and have a population of 47 million without health insurance is a shame. I don't think the Republicans will ever do anything about that kind of thing.

My grandfather was a Cuban patriot. He fought in the War of Independence against Spain. He was a major general during the war and after the war was a member of the constitutional assembly and held other government posts. But he was a populist who never profited from his times of notoriety or his times in government. Though my father was never in politics—he was an executive with a successful enterprise in Havana—he too was a very generous and a very honest person.

Originally I came to the United States with the influx of Cubans in 1961 at the early stages of what is called the Cuban exile saga. I came with my brother and my sister. At that time we didn't have papers. We had student visas. But the way it worked those days, it was not really an issue.

The impression that most Cubans are Republicans goes back to the fiasco of the Bay of Pigs. The older Cubans blame the Democrats; but just because Kennedy was president at the time, this does not necessarily reflect the facts. The invasion was primarily conceived and planned by the CIA during the last years of the Eisenhower administration. Many of the Cubans in that first influx to the United States were from the higher echelons—the business sector and professionals. Perhaps they thought the Republicans would be more responsive to their interests. Plus, there have been many individuals who have used the Castro-U.S. animosity to build their own interests, radio stations and the like. They live from that conflict. If you think about it, Cubans speaks with their pocketbooks much more strongly than they speak with their votes. Politically, they may be supporting Republicans, but the second largest source of hard currency in Cuba is remittances from Cuban exiles. Think of that as a vote, how significant that could be, if properly directed—instead of sticking to what has proven to be a failed policy. Restrictions in travel may at one point have been sensible and reasonable, but nowadays it's just a matter of, "I won't move until you move." In the end, it's to the advantage of Castro's regime to maintain the embargo. It gives them an excuse for the failure their economic system has turned out to be.

I don't know what the numbers will show in the next election. I sense from my conversations with other Cuban Americans that a lot of people are going to vote for the Democratic candidate. It's a sort of mystery to me, why so many Cubans are Republicans. Since the majority of them are immigrants—and having gone through the struggles of the immigrant—you would think they could see that the party that would represent their interests would be the Democrats.

Rosita Worl

Alaska

Dr. Rosita Worl, of Juneau, Alaska, is president of the Sealaska
Heritage Foundation, vice chair of the Sealaska Corporation, and
member of the board of the Alaska Federation of Natives. She
also teaches anthropology at the University of Alaska Southeast.

I'm very fortunate in that my mother took charge of my education. Though she had gone to school only through the sixth grade,
she possessed great wisdom and a strong sense of justice. She was
a union organizer and a civil rights advocate for Alaska Native
People during the 1950s when discriminatory practices were common—and commonly accepted. She thought that my education
would be greatly enhanced by traveling with her throughout
Southeast Alaska communities to attend her union meetings and
to record the minutes, at the expense of missing school. I also ac-
companied her to meetings with Governor Ernest Gruening to
protest the discriminatory practices against people of color. At the
tender age of sixteen, I learned very quickly and saw firsthand that
our poverty, our working conditions, and our segregated status in
the school system were not unique to our family but extended to
a class of people. I learned—without my mother having to tell
me—that it was the Democratic Party that was sympathetic and

that responded to our cause in seeking social and economic equity and in overcoming our oppressed condition.

Later, she emphasized to me that it was important that I remain a Democrat, and not switch parties even if the Democrats were not in the political majority in the Territorial Legislature or Congress. I'm not too certain that at that time I understood her rationale, but as I became involved in political advocacy on my own, I learned that it was the philosophy of the Democrats that drew and held my mother and that would also sustain me through the years. Even now, when it is apparent to me that the other political party might be better suited and supportive of the needs of the corporate world in which I now find myself, I remain a Democrat.

John TeKippe

Iowa

John TeKippe has been a firefighter since 1993. He is captain of
Engine Company 4 in Des Moines, and president of Local 4 of the
International Association of Fire Fighters.

What was the political situation in your family?

My parents are both Democrats, but now most of my siblings are
Republican. There are four boys and a girl. My three brothers are
Republicans, and my sister and I are Democrats.

How did that happen?

The joke is that they had such a good life as Democrats growing
up that they *thought* they were Republicans.

Why are you a Democrat?

I look at two things. One is family influence, primarily my dad.
And the other is the Roman Catholic Church. I grew up Catholic,
and still am. The one thing you always hear from the Knights of
Columbus or the Church itself is the phrase, "Faith without works
is dead." Social justice is a big part of the Catholic Church. If you

look at the political parties, the party that tends to want to build in safety nets and bring people up out of poverty is the Democratic Party, as opposed to the attitude of, "You have to fend for yourself, and if you don't make it, too bad," which is the message I frequently get from the Republican Party.

Certainly a lot of union members are Democrats. What about firefighters?
I think firefighters are probably the most conservative labor group. We may even have more registered Republicans than Democrats.

Why?
I think it's a mix of things. I'm a navy veteran. A lot of veterans go into public safety when they get out of the service, and many are Republicans. We also have a ton of sportsmen, gun enthusiasts. Second Amendment rights are a big deal with firefighters because of their off-duty hobbies.

Do you hunt?
I hunted as a kid growing up. My dad hunts. I probably still would if I was living where I grew up, in Northeast Iowa. I just don't have time for it. I'm too busy with family and being union president. I have to prioritize.

But if you and your dad are Democrats, and you hunt, or at least don't have anything against it, how does that fit with the stereotype that all sportsmen are Republicans?
That frequently comes up. The last few years the firefighters and labor put together a union sportsman club, as a more labor-friendly version of the NRA. I don't know that I'm moderate, but I'm certainly pragmatic. I don't care what kind of gun you own, as long as it's registered. And some guns do need to be made safer.

If you had to come up with one word or phrase or concept that says "Democrat," what would it be?

Collective bargaining. Nearly all the success we have had with pay and benefits has come out of the collective bargaining structure. When people are levelheaded, it works. There are parallels to the way we do things at church—fair play, a level playing field, that kind of thing. So yesterday and later on today and tomorrow, I put, or I will put, that collective bargaining tool to work to handle several kinds of problems, either with individuals or the group. That is my tool every day, and that is also the mantra of the Democratic Party.

Do you recall anything significant about a specific election?

I remember when Nixon resigned, even though I was pretty young—I was born in 1967. Nixon was giving a speech on TV. I knew my family were diehard Democrats, and as a kid, you know what bothers your parents. And so I knew the guy on TV was one of the *other* guys. When I asked my dad what this guy on TV was doing, he could have spun it pretty hard, but he said, "He made a mistake and he's telling us about it." I always liked that. My parents have never been hard partisans. They have a belief structure politically that they really follow, but they have never been people who tear down the other side. I think about that frequently when I get into an argument with somebody, on some labor or political thing, I think: how am I going to conduct myself, like that example, or like the example of what I *don't* want to be—the hard, partisan, ugly, fighting person.

Do you think the Democrats personify that more?

I think the Democrats I *like* personify that more. I think both parties don't do a good enough job of being that way. Too much is about the headlines and not enough about the work. In Iowa we have a caucus structure for the presidential process. It's not like other states where people vote individually. The caucus structure is a conversation, it's about voting in groups. A person who is successful in caucuses is someone who is able to talk to people with different opinions and convince them that they should be comfortable caucusing for that person's candidate. When someone can work that way within a group, they're the most successful.

The Party of the
Reluctant-but-Registered

If a political party can be thought of as a family, these Democrats are not thrilled about going home for the holidays this year. They are registered as Democrats, and they will likely vote for Democratic candidates, but they are not wholly pleased with the Party and its leadership. Though a segment of the American population has always been wary of politicians of all kinds, and of the compromises inevitably made during the political process, Richard Nixon and Watergate can be credited with turning the raised eyebrow into a universal expression. The 2000 elections served to reinforce a feeling of frustration and cynicism throughout a large segment of voters. Reluctant-but-registered Democrats believe in the principles that underscore the Party, but feel that Democratic politicians don't do enough to uphold them. Given their ambivalence, why don't they register Independent? Because they can't vote in the primaries and because they realize that with a system balanced by two behemoths, it is simply better to stand with one side.

Camilo José Vergara

New York

Camilo José Vergara, a writer and photographer, was born in Chile and moved to the United States in 1965. He has been the recipient of numerous awards, including a MacArthur "genius" Fellowship. His most recent book is *How the Other Half Worships*.

Tell me why you're a Democrat.

Because I'm not a Republican. The other choice is just too terrible, for me it will be four more years of political alienation. When I became a U.S. citizen in the late 1970s, I would vote the entire Socialist and Communist line, and then I would look behind me to see if the FBI was spying. But I soon got tired of doing this because I realized that it was an empty gesture.

What does "Democrat" mean?

It's a little less bad. It means we are probably getting out of Iraq in three years rather than five. It means maybe the housing support programs will grow a little bit, that there may be some chance that some weak form of a universal health care may be implemented. Some tax loopholes for the rich and the superrich may be closed; the air, the land, and the water may be better protected; and energy consumption may be kept at bay or perhaps even decreased.

We may be blessed with a ruling elite that shows a friendlier and less arrogant face to the rest of the world, one that is less likely to go to war. The choice between Republicans and Democrats is really limiting: two choices that are very much alike—except that with one, the Democrats, you have a tiny bit of hope, a tiny ray that comes out of the cracks.

In your work, you have documented a lot of low-income, poverty-stricken areas. How do the Democrats relate to those environments?

Nobody really seems to care much about those places, but at least ghettos are part of the Democrats' vision. They are certainly not part of the vision of the Republican Party.

Okay, so you're not the most enthusiastic Democrat, but still, you remain a Democrat. What would the party need to do to get you more enthusiastic?

First of all is the overriding concern with the situation in Iraq. I think they just should pull out, and pull out the safest possible way, but pull out everything as quickly as they can. I want so badly to live in a peaceful country. I would like to see a health care system that reaches everybody effectively, and also to see subsidies to allow people of modest resources to pay for housing in places like New York, or Chicago, or L.A. And I don't mean only for destitute people to live there, although they are part of it, but I mean people like, schoolteachers. My son was teaching grade school in New York, and he was making twenty-nine thousand dollars a year. Where can you live on that money?

Tama Janowitz

New York

Tama Janowitz is the author of eight works of fiction (including her new novel, *They Is Us*), one book of nonfiction, and a book for children. Her writing has appeared in many journals and magazines, including *Vogue*, *Elle*, and the *New York Times Sunday Magazine*.

Elect Me President

I know little about democracy. I do not know much about what the Democratic Party stands for. In school I received little political information or instruction. Nevertheless, I believe that as a Democrat, if elected, things will be better.

Many of my values are closer to what politicians in the Democratic Party pretend to represent than the Republicans, although I do know that originally the Republicans were Democrats. Also, originally the Ku Klux Klan used to be good guys! And that Oliver Stone made a movie about the FBI rushing in to rescue civil rights workers in the South, which in my memory was quite different. And that once something is in a movie, we hold it to be a truth self-evident, but facts in a book are not necessarily.

Folks, this ain't de Tocqueville talking to you. I am a born American, to paraphrase Bellow's Augie March, practically uneducated, politically illiterate, but allowed to say what I want even though my dad did have a three-hundred-page secret dossier from when the FBI followed him around in the late '50s and early '60s at the taxpayer's expense.

MY BELIEFS

Just as there are people who believe that every American should have a right to bear arms to kill others if they have to or want to, but also that women should not be able to have abortions because they feel it is killing a human, I have my beliefs!

Here is what I do believe. That every time a bomb, a gun, a weapon, or a bullet is made, a white Republican American male gets richer.

Some of these guys make the weapons, and the taxpayer pays for it.

Other guys go and shoot off the weaponry. While these guys might be Republican, they do not get richer, because they die or have to go to Walter Reed Army Medical Center, which is a military hospital and which when my dad was in the army, back in the '50s, was known to be terrible.

Other men have to come back and rebuild what was blown up and these are known as contractors. The actual people who do the rebuilding are poor people, usually unskilled laborers, who, according to the Republicans, should not be allowed into our country.

But at least if they are in their own blown-up country, we can offer them low-paying jobs rebuilding what we blew up and pay for it out of their own money, not ours, because they have corrupt governments who are already in debt to us.

Last but not least, I believe that every sperm in a man's ejaculate is one half of a human life, and therefore all the men who are against abortion must not ejaculate unless they can find enough fertile eggs so that each and every eensy-weensy motile tadpole will be able to survive.

I know some other things about Republicans, who are not that much different than Democrats, but in this limited space let me state that it is the Republicans who cut down virginal forests, which has left me with many stumps on the campaign trail.

IF ELECTED

If I am elected president or given an all-powerful position, here is what I will do: I will take every man on the Supreme Court and I will impregnate him.

Some will be impregnated by rape; some will be impregnated lovingly but genetic testing will prove their children will be serial killers who need a great deal of expensive plastic surgery. And there will be no health insurance for these pregnant justices, let alone any stem cell research for when they get Alzheimer's.

I will make sure to take away the judges' money and their friends and any support from their family. And I will say to them as I say to you today, either you carry this unwanted child to term or find a backstreet abortionist.

And then I will give their babies—after they are born but need frequent diaper changes!—to a bunch of other white men who do not make the laws but who are anti-abortion.

And from them I shall take *their* money and friends and make them raise the babies by themselves in a world without diapers disposable, nor diapers of cloth, or at least if I do decide to permit diapers of cloth they ain't going to have the money for no diaper service to come and take the dirty nappies away.

IN CONCLUSION

In conclusion, for the most part, I cannot and will not say what I intend to do after I am elected. Nor will I say what is good about Democrats.

But I can express, in part, what is wrong with the other party, who in this present time is the party of the first part. And I will say that I will be very busy undoing damages and making sure there is never again a Bay of Pigs or a Cuban missile crisis—or wait, was that something to do with Democrats?

Jonathan Franzen

New York

Jonathan Franzen is the author of the novels *The Corrections*,
Strong Motion, and *The Twenty-Seventh City*; a collection of essays,
How To Be Alone; and a memoir, *The Discomfort Zone*.

I'm sorry I'm late in writing my reasons "Why I'm a Democrat."
I was on the road for two weeks, and then I got a bad cold. But
even aside from this, I'm having trouble with the assignment. I
know that nothing spectacular is called for and that I shouldn't
stare too hard at the problem. But I really can't think of what to
say. I had an idea involving a C. S. Lewis novel, *Prince Caspian*,
in which a rainbow coalition of lovable misfits defeats a corrupt,
militarized, conformist regime through its superior faith and good-
ness, but when I wrote it down it sounded sentimental and unreal-
istic. The actual reasons I'm a Democrat are so familiar and widely
shared that it seems almost pointless to name them. They include:
my hatred of Republicanism (especially in its current rage-filled,
fear-mongering, lie-spreading instantiation), my belief in the
power of good government, my wish to pay my fair share of taxes,
my sympathy for underdogs of all kinds, and my love of nature
and big cities. The usual prosaic shopping list. The fact is, I don't
have any particularly colorful history with the Democratic Party.

My parents usually voted for the Democrat but they never called themselves Democrats. And it's not in my nature to get excited about platforms or candidates, even if I'm reasonably sympathetic to them, because the rhetoric of campaigning is necessarily so simplistic. Basically, I'm a Democrat because the Democratic Party is the only mainstream choice available to a leftist intellectual like me. If I thought the Republicans would do a better job of protecting nature—not very likely, I know!—I would probably switch parties. So there's a conviction deficit here, an enthusiasm deficit; and writing an encomium is very hard in the face of such a deficit. Still, I'm a Democrat and I'm likely to remain one. If the party could attract a new crop of smart, sophisticated candidates in the mold of Jim Webb and Al Gore (post-2000), and Henry Waxman, I might even get excited.

The Everything Party

A publication containing chapters for each and every reason Democrats are Democrats would require multiple volumes. Suffice it to say, each member of the Democratic Party has more than one reason for belonging to the party. Some of those reasons were mentioned repeatedly by nearly all contributors to this book; at the same time, each contributor has reasons unique to and shaped by his or her personal experiences. More than one contributor to this book described becoming a Democrat after learning to think for themselves. Ultimately, the Democrats are the party of open minds.

Carl Mehling

New York

Paleontologist Carl Mehling is a collections manager at the American Museum of Natural History in New York City.

Ideally, Democrats allow and embrace change and diversity. I've been of that general mind my entire life. I like to question everything, even myself. Just accepting certain ideas is kind of like death. Since I see things from an evolutionary perspective, anything that stays still for too long is going to go extinct. Conformity = stasis = death. Everything has to change with time, especially thinking.

It's ridiculous to think that you can divide the thoughts of millions of people into two categories, when there are always shades of everything along the way, like a spectrum, but I would assume that the scientific community is more Democratic. That's the feeling I get, but then again, I do live in New York. The way science works is certainly more in line with the way the Democrats view issues related to science—stem cell research and the environment and that kind of thing. Science questions everything.

Ideological freedom recognizes that one might not have it all correct or figured out—this is why I favor science over dogma. In fact, diversity, in all its forms, is favorable since it has a better chance of containing the best way of doing things. Allowing change and diversity allows the possibility of truth. I find "questioning" the most important and admirable of human qualities. Nearly everything we have ever learned was born with a question.

One problem that emerges is that politicians must have utter conviction in order to prevail. Philosophically, the twain shall never meet. So, while I'm not going to say that Democrats are never intransigent on one topic or another, I do feel that they are more open to diverse ways to thinking.

The Democrats seem to me more concerned with humanity as a whole, and the environment and the bigger picture instead of their own existence and their own portion of the world. With science, it's not just one person or dogma coming up with something scary, like global warming. Once an idea is in the hands of the scientific community, whose only "dogma" is its methodology, it gains an independent truth. It's not one person's or one dogma's agenda. It's the whole diverse community.

In the end, I don't think that I (and maybe no one) "chose" to be one party or another. We just become aware at some point that there are terms people use to label themselves, and we pick one that best fits who we already are, whether by nature or nurture is another question altogether. To dream that the sum of American thought can be split into two sections, neatly in opposition, is as simple-minded as it is dangerous. But I guess for now, we have to work with what we have. And I am a Democrat.

Paul Weitz

California

Paul Weitz is a writer-director whose credits include *In Good Company*, *American Dreamz*, *American Pie*, and *About a Boy*, for which he received an Academy Award nomination.

Why I'm a Democrat:

When a Democrat lies under oath it's about oral sex.

I like having a president who knows there's only one "u" in "nuclear."

I'd rather be Barney Frank than Larry Craig.

I don't want to let religious fundamentalists have nuclear weapons.

Lincoln was a Democrat—oh wait, he was a Republican? What happened to the Republican Party?

Libby Yarborough
South Carolina

Libby Yarborough is a real estate broker in Greenville, South
Carolina, where she grew up. In the late 1960s and early '70s,
after earning a political science degree, she was employed for
several years in congressional offices in Washington, D.C.

What's it like being a Democrat in the South these days?
Lonely! There are not that many of us left.

Why is that?
I'm sure you're aware that the "Solid South" was at one time a
major voting bloc for the Democratic Party. That was before
civil rights legislation became a major priority for the national
Democratic Party. With the beginning of civil rights reform during John Kennedy's presidency, and the enactment of major legislation when President Johnson was in office, the South began to
pull away from the party, especially at the national level. Forced
integration of public schools was a major issue that was opposed by
a large portion of the Southern population. Unfortunately, some
Southern politicians attempted to take advantage of all the con-
troversy to advance their own careers, or even just to stay in office. Many of them became Republicans, and over the years, the

process has escalated. Both Kennedy and Johnson were aware that the Democrats would lose the "Solid South" by pushing for civil rights, and they did. But there is no question that America is a better place because of those reforms.

But that was forty years ago.

That's true, but many Southerners now identify with the Republican Party for other reasons. Fiscal conservatives in the South, as well as those who are conservative on cultural and social issues, tend to identify with the Republican Party. Many Southern voters take a very conservative approach to government in general. A common refrain is "just get the government off our backs."

The religious right also plays a large role in the Republican Party in the South. They like to identify the Democratic Party as being controlled by wealthy Hollywood donors. And conservative voters tend to see Hollywood and the media as being responsible for the decline in moral values in younger Americans. American culture *has* been coarsened—they're right about that. But I see the decline in moral values as more related to the demise of a strong, cohesive family structure than as a political issue.

You said you once worked for a Republican on Capitol Hill.

I did. Glenard P. Lipscomb. He was a Republican congressman from California. He was not a way-out conservative. He was a fine man of wonderful character who was ethical in every way, really more of an old-style Republican—one who put country above party. His closest friends in Congress were Gerald Ford and Melvin Laird, both of whom were also very fine, highly principled men. It was a Democratic congressman—my congressman from home at that time, Robert Ashmore, a conservative Democrat—who helped me get the job with Mr. Lipscomb. I wonder if you'd see that kind of cooperation today. After Mr. Lipscomb passed away at a very young age, I moved back to South Carolina to work for Governor John West, who was a progressive Democrat.

Why are you a Democrat?

An important influence was my grandmother, who would come up to visit us every year from Florida for the month of August. She was a devoted Democrat, a tremendous admirer of Eleanor Roosevelt and Adlai Stevenson. Even though we were only of grammar school age, my brother, Danny, and I loved to spend entire days with Grandmother glued to the TV watching the Democratic and Republican conventions. It was clear to me early on that the Democratic Party took an active role in trying to improve the quality of life for people. They stepped in and took action. When you look back at all the important legislation that has been passed in the last century—legislation that has helped people—from Social Security to Medicare reform to, well, all of it! Any important legislation that improved life for the average American was advanced by Democrats and in many cases, opposed by Republicans. Here's an example: when I first started selling real estate, a woman—even if she had a great job—could not quality for a mortgage loan without a man cosigning. I had a client who had recently been divorced from a prominent local doctor, so she was looking for a house in which to start a new life. Even though she was financially qualified based on her own income, the bank told her that her ex-husband would have to cosign the note and the mortgage. You can imagine what we had to go through to get the ex-husband to agree to do this for her, and I will never forget how demeaning it was for my client. The banks were able to discriminate until Democrats took the initiative and enacted legislation to protect the rights of women, just as they had done earlier in fighting for civil rights for minorities. Throughout my life, I have seen the Democrats take an active role in solving problems and improving the quality of life for everyone.

Why haven't more Southern Republicans come to realize that it's the Democrats who are working for them?

I simply do not understand it. I have had two repair people working in my house recently. They are both people who have benefited from legislation passed by Democrats, but they are rabid Republicans. From our conversations, I think it's mostly connected to issues of social conservatism. When I asked the serviceman who was repairing my gas oven who he was going to vote for, he said the last person in the world he would vote for is Hillary Clinton, or Barack Obama. He specifically mentioned the behavior of Britney Spears, which he thought was disgusting because she has little children. He seemed to think the Democratic candidates shared Britney's values since it has been so widely reported that they get money from Hollywood donors.

I'll bet anything Britney Spears is a Republican!

Who knows? But I think the fact that large donations from people in Hollywood often go to Democratic candidates has caused people who are socially conservative to lump all the Democratic candidates into that "Hollywood influence" category.

Then I had a plumber working on my house who hates any intervention of the government into our lives—which he associates with the Democratic Party. When I asked him for an example, he was quick to criticize Al Gore for the enactment of legislation that resulted in the infamous low-flow toilets, which do not work. Also, he said the low-flow shower heads make it impossible to have a good shower anymore! Of course, this legislation was passed to help conserve water, which is a dwindling resource especially here in the Southeast, where we have had a major drought with mandatory restrictions in some places. But, according to my Republican plumber friend, the legislation was enacted before manufacturers had time to redesign the toilets to flush properly with the lower flow requirements.

Do you still work for Democratic candidates as a volunteer?

Yes, I have always taken an active role in politics.

What's that like now, to work on Democratic campaigns in South Carolina?

It can be really discouraging. We had one Democrat win in the recent city council elections because she represents a mostly African American district. But the other Democratic candidates lost. That's the situation with the Democratic Party now in South Carolina. Our largest base is the African American community, and sometimes their voter turnout is not as large as that of the conservative, religious-right segment of the population. The Republicans *always* turn out to vote. Greenville is the home of Bob Jones University, which is a real right-wing conservative institution, and it's very influential locally.

Have you sold any houses to people from Bob Jones University?

We sell to anybody and everybody. And some of those people are delightful. They are some of the hardest-working people, and they contribute a lot to the community. But their approach to politics baffles me. I have always had a hard time understanding how really religious people can rationalize being Republicans. My family always felt that giving money to the Democratic Party was almost as good as giving money to the church.

What would you say to a neighbor who is not sure about which party to join?

I'm sure you have heard the expression, "You should dance with the one who brung you." To me, that explains why I'm a Democrat. You should vote for, and be loyal to, the party that is taking action to improve the quality of life for all people, not just the privileged few.

Craig Lesley

Oregon

Craig Lesley is the author of four novels, including *River Song* and *The Sky Fisherman;* a memoir, *Burning Fence: A Western Memoir of Fatherhood*, and numerous other works. The recipient of several national fellowships and literary awards, he is the Senior Writer-in-Residence at Portland State University.

I grew up in Eastern Oregon, country where Democrats are as rare as albino elk. During my childhood, Eisenhower was hailed as the Second Coming and FDR was the Antichrist. I was steeped in the culture of cattle, timber, and Republicans. Senator Wayne Morse, the outspoken Democratic "Tiger in the Senate" was viewed as a Communist.

Fortunately, my mother—a single, working parent—insisted that I attend college, and I was fortunate enough to receive a full-ride academic scholarship to Whitman College. In those days, Whitman was conservative, Walla Walla (Washington, where it is located) ultra-conservative, but in classes and discussion groups, I learned other ways of thinking. These were the tumultuous years of civil rights demonstrations, escalation of the war in Vietnam, the beginnings of the women's rights movement.

As I listened to the lectures in history and political science classes, I began to see that the Democratic Party had a lot to offer someone like myself who grew up working class. Too, I began to notice that many of the people who became Peace Corps volunteers, as well as those who left college for a year to help blacks in the South register to vote, came from the Young Democrats at Whitman.

In graduate school at the University of Kansas, I hung out with the liberal fringe. Those of us who taught freshman English made a pact not to flunk freshman men for fear that they would be drafted immediately. (The school had an unwritten policy to flunk out one-fifth of the freshman.)

We held antiwar protests and civil rights demonstrations in conservative Lawrence. We pushed and the town and university pushed back. I came to understand that the university itself was part of the military-industrial complex, that large grants from conservative organizations shaped university decisions.

I studiously followed the "other" war, Johnson's War on Poverty, and most of the decisions in that war were intended to help the same people I wanted to help through teaching or by other means.

When George McGovern ran for office, I worked vigorously for his campaign, along with other young idealists, old union workers, professional politicos. Even though he didn't win, campaigning gave me a terrific high. I knew I was on the right side.

In all my novels, I write about working-class people, those that Democratic policies are most likely to help. I believe Jimmy Carter was a great president and I admired his wife's work with children. Her book, *First Lady from Plains*, and my novel, *Winterkill*, were published by Houghton Mifflin in the same month, and Rosalyn and I had a good chance to talk at a sales meeting in Boston. I was a big supporter of Clinton, too, and had a nice note from the Oval Office saying he had enjoyed my third novel, *The Sky Fisherman*. A week later, the Monica scandal broke, but Clinton's policies stayed pretty much intact.

The Democratic Party has shaped my views, values, and beliefs. In their policies lie the best hopes for the working class, the minority, the marginalized, the sick, the mentally ill.

For the time being, rascals and thugs occupy the White House, but I look forward to the day this county elects a decent president, woman or man.

Olympia Vernon

Louisiana

Olympia Vernon, of Hammond, Louisiana, is the author of three critically acclaimed novels: *Eden*, which won the 2004 American Academy of Arts and Letters' Rosenthal Foundation Award; *Logic*, which was nominated for the Mississippi Institute of Arts and Letters Award; and *A Killing in This Town*, a *New York Times* Editors' Choice and winner of the first Ernest J. Gaines Award for Literary Excellence. She is currently the Hallie Brown Ford Chair at Willamette University.

The Umbilical Cord

They shot that man in the motorcade and his wife held his head together.

His head sloped forward, aside, into the pink of her skirt.

I could not forget the leaning of his shoulder, as if sleep had overcome him, as if he had been shaped by the quiet fertility of an umbilical cord.

He slept there—on the pink—the lungs of the world; the crying out; the Universe; all had kept their noise heard upon this death.

I had drawn a photo of him on an envelope; his hair was parted, as it had been in the paper; the jaw—what a strict, unyielding bone it was—had crumbled under lead; how could I have pictured it with a bullet in it? With blood?

I had heard or read somewhere that protection had been offered him, but he rejected it.

I had not cared, before viewing the footage of this, this murder—before him and other hims like him—about the business of Democrats and Republicans. It was all so silly, you see. This business of elephants and donkeys.

There were wars; poverty; homelessness; countries of war and poverty and homelessness and starvation and mutilated women and children starving and dying and blood; there was blood in America—yes, there . . . was . . . blood . . . in . . . America.

When I thought of this, I thought of the list I had begun to compile of those who had fought against war and poverty and homelessness and starvation and blood in America and elsewhere: I knew not whether they were Democrats or not, but they had all borne the same Eye—the same nerve and line—and I had seen that Eye in footage and photographs of JFK and Martin Luther King, Jr. and Viola Liuzzo and Jimmy Carter and my Mama and hers and my stepfather—he told me once that we were Democrats because we were black—and his folks and Shirley Chisholm and everyone I knew in my neighborhood of Mt. Hermon, Louisiana, and, too, Osyka, Mississippi.

We were Democrats because we were black, he said . . . and then I later saw footage of JFK's shoulder and the blood that was his . . . and I thought of the business of animals and what elephants do . . . trample; overpower; crush . . . me.

Not only JFK . . . but Martin Luther King, Jr.'s shoulder, I thought of his shoulder, how it had sloped and died—and Viola

Liuzzo's shoulder. I wanted to be a part of that shoulder. I wanted to be a part of what I had read and heard and sensed: I wanted to be a part of the business of Democrats . . . what torch had been lit by them . . . the Kennedys; Jimmy Carter; King; Jackson; Liuzzo; my folks and their folks who were against the murders of the Rubin Stacys; the Leo Franks; the Schwerners, the Goodmans, the Chaneys; the Charles Moores and Henry Dees . . . I wanted to be a part of the business of Democrats.

For I had drawn a photo of Us on an envelope with one jaw; one unyielding bone.

And there was no bullet.

No blood.

William Wegman

New York and Maine

William Wegman's art encompasses photography, painting, drawing, collage, and video. His work is collected in numerous books and other publications and was the subject of Funney/ Strange, a recent retrospective exhibition at the Brooklyn Museum, the Smithsonian American Art Museum, and other major arts institutions.

William Wegman
Possibly Bright
Ink and/or Gouache on Silver Gelatin Print
11 ¼ x 10 inches
3193

★10★

The Party of
Ex–Grand Old Party-ers

People who take the time and the trouble to switch from one belief system to another tend to be passionate about those beliefs. Which means that former Republicans sometimes turn out to be the most enthusiastic Democrats. They didn't fall into or grow up with their political affiliation. They actively chose it after belonging to the Republican Party (or, in one case recounted here, the College Republicans) and determining that the Republican way of doing things is in opposition to their manner of thinking and living. After careful consideration, for different reasons, and at different times in their lives, all seven of these Republicans became Democrats.

Four of the seven are from the same county in Oregon, where I lived for a couple of years in the early 1990s. They are a case study on their own, one that illustrates the inherent unreliability of political stereotypes. Wallowa County, in the far northeastern corner of Oregon, is quintessentially rugged and rural Western territory. Forty years ago, the majority of its registered voters were Democrats, including many of the area's cattle ranchers. In the years since, land-use law viewed as restrictive persuaded many of those Democrats to change parties, and the Republicans have become the majority. Still, the Democrats in the area are alive and active. Of the four profiled here—all people I have known for years—I assumed two were life-long Democrats and was surprised to learn of their Republican pasts. The other two, I wasn't sure about, but forced to guess, I probably would have said they were Republicans. I was half right in that they used to be.

Lee Papa

New York

Lee Papa's blog, the Rude Pundit, can be read daily at rudepundit
.blogspot.com. Papa is a playwright and professor of drama studies at the College of Staten Island / CUNY. He has performed
his one-person plays, based on the blog, in New York City and
Calgary.

I was raised a poor white bigot. My Jewish grandmother scoffed at "the schwartzes." My brother would drive through black neighbor-hoods in my Louisiana city and, bizarrely, shake a plastic devil's pitchfork at families on their porches. My Italian father thought we should nuke Iran during the hostage crisis, that we should have nuked Vietnam, and that capital punishment should be broadcast on ABC's *Wide World of Sports*. For him, the worst of all were gay men—just pedophiles waiting to strike. He was worried sick that his bookish, theatre-loving son was gonna be some craven sword swallower or something.

So I went away to college, Tulane University, rock solid in my hawkish, Reagan-worshipping, gay-fearing Neanderthal retarda-tion. And, beyond the immersion in cultures and races outside of my narrow purview, I took a course in political philosophy with Professor Jean Danielson. We read Hobbes and Locke, and I began to think that maybe the world didn't need to be this brutish place, filled with isolated people who condemned others for their existence. By the time we got to Rousseau and by the time I was going to the Desire housing project with a friend to have dinners at his aunt's apartment and by the time I was going to see REM and Frank Zappa in concert, I was in one of those full-blown existential crises that you get to go through if you pay attention at school.

Oh, and I was a member of the College Republicans. And it was 1984, and Ronald Reagan was going to win re-election. We'd sit around in each other's rooms and laugh at how Reagan seemed like he was kicking Walter Mondale's ass in debates. Between, you know, snorts of cocaine and sex with the pure conservative girls who lived on the floor below.

I was walking across campus with a dorm friend from Boston, heading to a November meeting of the College Republicans. He said to me, in a voice resonant of Thurston Howell III intonations, "I can't believe the Democrats want to stop the president from building more nuclear missiles. We have to keep up with the Soviets, don't you think?"

In one of those rare, startling moments of complete clarity, I stopped in my tracks and slowly said, "No. No, I think we have enough nukes." Thurston stared at me, quizzically, perhaps waiting for the punch line. I continued, "I don't think I can go to this meeting." I turned around, headed back to my dorm, quit the College Republicans, and joined the newspaper to do investigative reporting. Luckily, I was only seventeen, so I couldn't vote. I would have voted for Reagan, and that's karma I've been working off for a long, long time.

People change. When I turned eighteen, I registered to vote as a Democrat and never looked back. My mother and sister voted for Clinton, Gore, and Kerry. My formerly Limbaugh-listening brother recently decided that George W. Bush can shove his war.

Shortly after he died, I found out my father pretended illness to get out of the draft. Oh, and his best friend was gay. Yeah, he'd go dancing at gay clubs with him.

Goddamn Republicans. They're nothing if not consistent.

Elliot Anderson

Nevada

A machine gunner in the U.S. Marine Corps, Sergeant Elliot Anderson has been deployed overseas three times, including to Afghanistan in 2004 and 2005. Currently on individual ready reserve—from which he could be deployed again—he is studying political science at the University of Nevada, Las Vegas, while dealing craps at Hooters Hotel and Casino.

If you were raised in Wisconsin by parents who were Democrats, why did you not consider yourself a Democrat at first?

To me there was a very clear reason I didn't consider myself a Democrat. I believed the lies the Republican Party put through the media about the Democratic Party. They did a real effective job convincing everyone the Democratic Party "hated the military." For this reason, after I signed on with the Marines, I considered myself a moderate Republican. Still, many of my positions on other issues fell on the Democratic side of things.

What changed your mind?

Hurricane Katrina was a bit of a watershed moment for me. The natural process in the military is to give your leaders (including elected leaders) the benefit of the doubt. After I saw President

Bush tell FEMA commissioner Mike Brown he was doing a "heck of a job," I reevaluated his leadership on all issues and started volunteering for the Democratic Party. From being in the military, I knew the last refuge of a good leader was to say, "I messed up, and now I'm going to fix it." To see the president whitewash what were obviously massive failures on all levels of government as a "heck of a job," to me was completely irresponsible and disgusting. After I started working with the Democratic Party, I figured out in quick order that the Democrats did not hate the military as the media had told me for years, and on some level still try to do today.

What does it mean to you to be a Democrat?

Being a part of the Democratic Party means living up to the preamble of the Constitution, which starts with "We the People." Democrats are the party that cares for people who are suffering. Democrats are the party that invests in getting more people involved in the political process. Democrats are the party that stands up for individual workers against big business. Democrats are the ones who take care of individual members of the military (by making sure they have the best equipment) and veterans by giving the Veterans Administration the biggest budgets. Finally, Democrats are the ones who stand up for American values such as the Bill of Rights—they don't just talk and wave a flag. Being a Democrat is recognizing that the people are the sovereigns of our country, and we should base our country on this fact.

How do you explain the impression many people have that vets are Republicans?

A big part of the reason people believe the military is all Republican is because the Republican Party talks a good game. If you repeat something over and over people will believe it. This can be proved false by simply going over demographics. The military is a cross-section of society, not coming from one group. You have kids from the inner cities of Chicago, Los Angeles, and New York. You have kids from cities like San Francisco (hardly a conservative bastion). You have kids from union families. You have kids who join because their families have no money to put them through college. You have kids who are Hispanic or African American. Would any political analyst care to wager all of these groups are made out of Republicans?

In addition Republicans are great at gestures. They are great at putting together events that tug at the heart, but not so great at putting their money where their mouths are. They've brought us shortages in body armor, they've brought us disgusting conditions for our wounded at Walter Reed Army Medical Center, and they've brought us inadequate funding for the Veterans Administration. The military, like me, is catching on and going to the party that gives money to the individual troops on the ground. We've seen generals, captains, and sergeants disagree on the issues with the Republican Party. They have seen which party gives money to the troops and not to their defense contractor buddies like the Republican Party does.

Dominick Dunne

New York and Connecticut

Dominick Dunne, who began his career as a Hollywood producer, is a journalist and author. He has written six best-selling
novels and four works of nonfiction, including two collections of
his articles for *Vanity Fair*. He is also the host of *Power, Privilege
and Justice* on Court TV.

I'm in the midst of writing a memoir before I cool, and at eighty-
two years old, I am simply aghast at some of the opinions I used to
have in earlier parts of my life. When I was asked to write about
"Why I Am A Democrat," which I proudly am, I thought it was
a wonderful idea, but it brought up a lot of memories about my
political past that I had managed to erase. You see, I wasn't always
a Democrat. I was a total asshole at that other time in my life. I
was pretending to be someone I wasn't. The reason I wrote asshole characters so correctly in my novels is because I was such
an asshole myself. Among other things that seem strange today
is that I voted for Goldwater and worked for him. My wife and I
were on a team with Hedda Hopper, the Hollywood gossip columnist who wore big hats and who was so right-wing, and we went
to parades and held up signs for Goldwater for President. Even
more shaming is that I once headed up a group called Catholics

Against Kennedy. I cringe to write this. My life changed. I became a failure. I vanished from my own life. I lived poor. Being poor and being a failure was the best thing that could have happened to me. I realized that everything I had stood for during those years in Hollywood was mortifying. I didn't have to be talked into becoming a Democrat. I had simply become a Democrat. Just as I'm proud to be an American, I'm proud to be a Democrat.

Ralph Swinehart

Oregon

Ralph Swinehart is a consulting civil engineer. Along with running his company, Wallowa Mountain Engineering, Swinehart raises Rambouillet sheep on a small farm near Enterprise.

Why are you a Democrat?

Four years of Richard Nixon.

Did you always feel that way about Nixon?

No. People forget about Nixon's war on pollution. It was a big deal. In college, my thing was civil and sanitary engineering. I wanted to design sewage treatment plants. So I was pro-Nixon. I first registered as a Republican. I voted for Nixon in 1968, and if I'd been old enough, I would have voted for Goldwater in '64. Then I started to think for myself and became a Democrat. I did not vote for Nixon when he ran a second time.

Having something to compare them to, what do you like about the Democrats?

I think they're more oriented to what the general population would like to see happen in the country, as opposed to just what big business would like.

What do you expect from the Democrats in return for your vote?

What I would like to see is the Democrats pushing for universal health care. That would be an ideal—and I see the Democrats going more in that direction than the Republicans. Also, because I'm a fiscally conservative Democrat, I'd like to see them balance the budget.

How do you think the Republicans managed to get a reputation as "the money party," when practically every time they're in power, the country ends up in debt?

They lie better. They tell people exactly what they want to hear, very convincingly, then they do just the opposite.

You grew up in Idaho, not thought of as a blue state. Are you from a Republican family?

My dad used to be a Roosevelt Democrat, but he's been a Republican for years now. We had a big ninetieth birthday party for him not long ago. Just to needle him, I said, "All the Republicans in the room, raise your hands." There were about thirty people there. Four hands went up.

Was he upset?

He was heartbroken. I'm kidding.

Ethel Chandler

Oregon

For twenty years, Ethel Chandler and her husband, Jim, owned and operated the Bed, Bread & Trail Inn in Joseph, Oregon.

I grew up a Republican, in Colville, Washington. My family was against the New Deal, even though they were quite poor. They thought people involved in the WPA weren't working that hard, that they were getting a handout. Many people with no skills were put in the WPA. It was more of a training really. You'd be going along, and you'd see men on the road in these WPA crews, leaning on their shovels. It got to be kind of a joke.

When I was married to my first husband, I was still a Republican. We had our own excavating business and bid on a lot of government contracts. When you are working on government contracts, there are lots of requirements. We were union, we paid the prevailing wage, and the men who worked for us had good benefits. It took quite a toll, the benefits. We didn't think the men realized what it cost us for health and welfare, and pension and all of that. Then came OSHA, which in hindsight was a good program, but it cost us even more. For example, we had to put a huge cage around our big excavating machine. It cost thousands of dollars.

When I got a divorce, I went back to school. One of the courses was political science. We had to take a test that asked if you were a Republican or a Democrat, and other questions about what you believed in. I was surprised how much I leaned toward the Democrats. Then I went to work for an outreach program at the church I belonged to—a Lutheran church in Gresham, Oregon. We had a kitchen to give food to people in need. It was during the Reagan administration when there were so many cuts in funding. Certain people who belonged to this church really resented the outreach program, for the same reasons my family was against the WPA: they felt the people receiving the food were just getting a handout. Some of the people who weren't happy were berry growers. They were looking at things the way I used to, from one side. When they complained, I would think: Do you provide transportation to the fields for your workers? Do you provide day care? Do you pay a living wage? Working in this program made me realize how few people are aware of the problems that go along with homelessness and poverty. Picking yourself up by your bootstraps is not always easy. That's when I become a Democrat.

Roland Johnson

Oregon

Roland Johnson has a private law practice in Enterprise, Oregon.

You're from a local farm family?

My family had a five-hundred-acre farm on Prairie Creek. We raised beef, hay, grain, and sheep. My great-grandfather came here in the early 1870s and settled in the lower valley, and my grandfather had the Temperance Creek Ranch in Hell's Canyon.

And they were traditionally Republicans?

Absolutely. In the old days, there were a lot of Democrats here who were ranchers, but my father and my relatives were always Republican. I started out that way. But being a Republican, being a conservative, didn't mean the same thing then that it does now.

What did it mean then?

There didn't seem to be a conflict between government regulating private enterprise for social purposes and the philosophy of the Republican Party. Nixon proposed a negative income tax. Republicans were for antitrust laws, if you can imagine that. Starting with Reagan, the party began pushing for laissez-faire economics. I never thought anything decent could come of laissez-faire economics in terms of a social situation we would desire. What does a business do in the absence of regulation? They go with what's profitable. The only way business is conducted with decent environmental restraints is through regulatory programs. That's how you avoid abusing people with too long working hours and exploiting children for labor, like they do in many underdeveloped countries. Most Republicans were somewhat comfortable with that, although typically, businessmen had to bear the cost of compliance, and sometimes it could be aggravating.

But many of them still saw the value of the compliance.

Yes, especially the regulations that affected somebody else. That's just human nature.

So what ultimately led you to switch parties?

I was a history student before I was a law student. I always viewed the impeachment proceedings against Andrew Johnson as a colossal mistake. I saw the whole thing unfolding again when they tried to impeach Clinton. That was the straw that broke the camel's back. That's when I became a Democrat.

Remind me of what the impeachment of Andrew Johnson involved.

They had no reason. Andrew Johnson was Lincoln's vice president, so he became president after the assassination, right after the close of the Civil War. The so-called "Radical Republicans"—and Lincoln was a Republican—were in control of Congress, and they disagreed with Johnson's Reconstruction policies. I'm not sure why they didn't like him, but they didn't like him, and they simply decided to impeach him. So the House of Representatives voted on Articles of Impeachment, and the Senate tried him, and was one vote shy of impeachment. It requires two-thirds of the vote in the Senate. So here we were again with Clinton. The very radical, fundamentalist Republicans voted on Articles of Impeachment in the House of Representatives, and Clinton was tried in the Senate, and was acquitted. I went down and changed my registration. I couldn't believe that here we were, over a hundred years later, repeating the same experience.

Was there anything else?

I had also become more uncomfortable with economic policies, with how wealth is distributed, and tax rates, and all that sort of thing. But the one thing that held me to the Republicans was their federal land management position. I thought the Democrats abandoned their constituency of blue-collar workers in favor of a liberal elite who didn't care whether the local economies in these federal land areas were destroyed. So people who were dependent upon the resource economies in rural areas became very disillusioned with the Democratic Party. The Democrats still don't do well in the West in any of those areas. On those kinds of issues, I agree with the Republicans a lot more. Wallowa, the little town where I live, is about ready to go down the tubes because they lost the last timber mill.

So even though you disagree with the Democrats on their environmental stance . . .

I don't disagree with *all* of their environmental policies. But some. People just don't understand. We want a very constructive, stand-improving harvest, which leaves the forests in better condition and does provide a resource and some use of land. They think out here we want to rape the forest land, but we don't.

Mary Hearing

Oregon

Before her retirement, Mary Hearing taught first and second graders in La Grande, Oregon. She has a vacation home at Wallowa Lake.

For more than fifty years, you were a Republican, and then this year you switched to the Democrats. What changed your mind?

Well, of course, the war, which is terrible. I think we've been lied to. Whether it's all the Republicans, I don't know. I think they whitewashed a lot of things. I don't like the idea of a whitewashing! I don't know how we'll get out of this mess.

So what does being a Democrat mean to you now? What do you think the word, or the party, stands for?

Hopefully, more honesty. More change for the good, for the better of our country. That's basically the reason I changed. I don't know that it makes that much difference, one vote.

But after what happened in 2000 in Florida, we saw that a small number of votes can make a huge difference.

That's true. I was very mad at myself. I didn't care for either one of them, and I ended up voting for Bush, which I've been worried about ever since.

Were you once involved in Republican politics? Your daughter, Elizabeth, remembered as a child having to go with you to pick up David Eisenhower at the airport for some event?

I wouldn't say I was all that involved. I did give a tea once for [GOP senator] Mark Hatfield's wife. A friend probably asked me to do it.

You said you haven't discussed switching registration with your friends who are Republicans. Say, in your bridge group, do you discuss politics?

No. I think two things to stay away from are religion and politics. Because it's up to the individual, their religion as well as their politics. So I would not mention to some of my friends that I have changed registration. Not that I'm ashamed of it, but I don't want to get into a discussion.

What do you expect from the Democratic Party in return for your vote?

To calm my fears about where this country is going.

★11★

The Party of the Future

Fact: research shows that Democrats are more likely to inspire hope than Republicans. It is a fact as far as the research for this book is concerned, in any case. These four Democrats, and one longtime resident who has considered becoming a citizen, have looked to the future. Though they don't view what may lie ahead with rose-colored lenses, they hope for better things, which they feel are more likely to come about with the Democrats in charge.

Irwin Redlener

New York

Dr. Irwin Redlener is a clinical professor of public health at Columbia University's Mailman School of Public Health and directs the school's National Center for Disaster Preparedness. He is also a Professor of Pediatrics at Columbia's College of Physicians and Surgeons and president and cofounder of the Children's Health Fund.

My first real job was running a VISTA program in East Arkansas. I was a twenty-six-year-old newly minted pediatrician who had responded to a VISTA poster and spent two years in what was then the sixth poorest county in the United States, Lee County, Arkansas. Ever since I began in health care—and I graduated from medical school in 1969—I have been focused on who actually has access to what in our society. The thing that drives my work as a child advocate is not so much a sense of charity, but a sense of justice. All of this is embodied in principles that the Democrats stand for, at least in my lifetime. Even before I had personal experience to draw on, there was the history of the Roosevelt and Truman administrations, all of which reinforced the notion that this was a party that at least cared about articulating a sense of justice and fairness. There is a caveat, however.

In the span of my career, from 1971 going forward, we have had every possible permutation—a Democratic president and a Republican Congress, a Republican president and a Democratic Congress and so on—all combinations. Even so, progress for children has generally been slow, no matter who has been in office. I've always had much more affinity for the language of Democrats than Republicans, but that has been slightly tempered by some sense of not getting enough even when Democrats have been in power. During my first summer in Arkansas I would actually tell people that I thought profound poverty in America and lack of access to health care within a decade would be old news, the problem would be solved. It was youthful naiveté. I was a Kennedy-Johnson kid, imbued with a sense of optimism and possibility. And here I am, thirty-six years later, and we're still struggling. The day you are speaking to me [October 3, 2007] is the day President Bush vetoed the children's health insurance program. This was a strong Democratic Congress, but it wasn't quite strong enough to override the veto.

What I thought about when I was twenty-six has been tempered by a lot of years of struggle, and I'm a little more despairing. But I have a son who just graduated medical school. When I look at him, I think maybe Michael's generation will more definitively see solutions to these challenges of poverty and access that sometimes seem intractable to me. All that said, I remain, very staunchly, a Democrat because in the Democratic Party lies the nation's best hope for achieving some of these larger goals that are so critical to the promises of justice and fairness that are the bedrock of our democracy.

Shahed Amanullah

Texas

Shahed Amanullah is a real estate developer in Austin. He
also develops websites for the Muslim community through
halalfire.com

Where are you from originally?

I was born in Hollywood, California, to parents who immigrated
in the 1960s from Chennai, India. I grew up in Orange County,
which was and is very Republican.

So why are you a Democrat?

I'm a Democrat because I believe that the values of the Democratic
Party most mirror my Muslim values, in terms of how we should
interact with those around us—with compassion, understanding,
and an eye toward social justice. Other, more socially conservative Muslims, may disagree, but I see no conflict between a strict
personal morality and a desire to ensure that all citizens have the
freedom to live their lives as they see fit.

In 2004 you were a cofounder of "Muslims for Kerry"? How did that come about?

I reserved the "muslimsforkerry.com" domain name and used it to organize Muslim support for his candidacy. There were a few other grassroots efforts going on within the Muslim community at the time. We combined forces and soon the Kerry campaign came knocking, assigning a staff member to provide support and help organize our volunteers to go from mosque to mosque in swing states as the election grew closer.

What were Bush's people doing in the Muslim community at that time?

They were doing something similar, although their efforts were more geared at targeting high net-worth individuals for donations rather than getting out the vote. They pretty much figured they weren't going to get the Muslim vote anyway.

Why?

With the discomfort the Muslim community had toward Bush's foreign policy and other things, it would have been a hard sell. They realized their efforts would be better spent elsewhere. Let's put it this way: in 2004, Muslims voters were not low-hanging fruit for the Bush campaign. To their credit, they didn't ignore the community entirely, but they mostly went after donations from wealthy individuals, which to me really emphasized the differences in the way the two parties operate. The Democrats are more about outreach to the grassroots. They want to get people involved. The Republicans are more about going to the people with power and money and trying to tap into them.

What did you hope to accomplish working for Kerry?

What I've been trying to do for years is to make the case that Democratic values are Muslim American values. You're probably aware that the Muslim community really voted en masse for Bush in 2000. A lot of Muslims are socially conservative, and because of that they felt comfortable with Bush and the Republicans, with the politics of judgment, both moral and political. But after 9/11 they realized that those same guns could be turned against them. They began reacting to criticism the same way a lot of socially liberal people do when they are castigated for certain behavior or beliefs: you don't even know me, how can you paint me with that kind of broad brush? After 9/11 a lot of Muslims realized that we have to join the party that includes us, not excludes us—the party that is for tolerance, for welcoming different views, the party that has compassion for outsiders. And that is the Democrats. Before 9/11 civil rights was never a Muslim issue, but after 9/11 we realized that civil rights meant something to us, and that one party cared about it and one party didn't.

How do you think the Republicans handle Muslims at this stage?

As a community, we are trying to get to a place where we are accepted as full citizens of this country and not as permanent outsiders. Republicans pay attention to Muslims if it involves money or influence or power—or connections to overseas businesses that can benefit them in some way. That's when we get their attention. But if you are really down and out—and Muslims were down and out after 9/11 when we were looked at with so much suspicion—it was the Democrats who stood up for us. It was the Democrats who said we are not going to sacrifice your civil rights for security. At

a time when it would have been really easy for everybody to say,
"You know something, we have to protect ourselves here, and we
can't take chances," the Democrats didn't abandon us.

*Can you think of any other experience you've had that validated your deci-
sion to become a Democrat?*

When I was in my mid-twenties—this was the mid-1990s—and
living in the San Francisco Bay area, I used to go to both the
Republican and Democratic state conventions.

Were you thinking of becoming a Republican?

No, I used to go to both conventions simply to push for inclusion
of Muslims in the political process. I was open to either party as
a vehicle for advancing our concerns. I thought there could be
equal access to both parties. Even though I have always been a
Democrat, I was tolerant of Muslims being Republicans because
I thought, well, that's not my personal political inclination, but
if some Muslims feel comfortable with that, that's fine. It wasn't
until after 9/11 that I took the gloves off and said, this is a fight for
the future of our country. Are my grandchildren going to feel like
they are part of this country, that they are properly American, or
that they are still outsiders?

So what happened at these state conventions?

We would set up these hospitality booths and talk to people about
the Muslim community and what it represented. At the Republican conventions, I remember I would talk about how Muslims
share the deep values of Republicans. What I got in response was
fairly blunt questions along the lines of: how much do you guys
donate to political campaigns? And I would go on talking, saying things like, well, as a community, right now we're trying to

get people involved, and the donations and all of that will come later. So at one point, someone—I don't remember the name, but someone pretty high up with the California Republican party— took me aside and said, bluntly, because I was a new guy trying to figure out whether we belonged with the Republicans—this person took me aside and said, "You're the only group of people that came here without money in hand, so don't think anyone is going to pay attention to you."

Then I went to the Democratic state convention. They actively advised us how to get Muslims involved in the party, and gave me information that was useful, the whole grassroots organizing thing. They did not tell me what the entry fee was.

Is there anything you don't like about the Democrats?

They need to become better at courting religious voters. They have Muslim support right now because Muslims find common cause due to civil rights issues. But Democrats need to become much more open about religious voters in general because Muslim voters have not left their religion behind. There is a place for strong religious people in the Democratic Party. And that needs to be cultivated.

But what about the separation of church and state? The recent emphasis on religion in political contests is antithetical to the organizing principles of the United States.

I don't mean incorporating religion into the public sphere. I mean courting religious voters. Just because Muslims feel strongly about their religion doesn't mean they can't find common cause with Democrats who feel strongly about other things. Here's an example—gay marriage. A lot of Muslims who are socially conservative might have said in the past that they oppose gay marriage. Now, there is a greater tendency for Muslims to look at it and say: if we tell them they can't marry, what's to prevent somebody from telling us that we can't practice our religion? We want to protect our religious rights, but at the same time we should be open-minded about letting others live their lives as they choose as long as it doesn't hurt anyone. I think there is a place for religious people to be in that sphere, in a place of tolerance. The Democrats can really make that case. It doesn't mean that any of us impose our beliefs on anyone else. We can build an America in which we all feel strongly about our specific beliefs, but we leave each other alone. That's the kind of society we want to build.

Kenneth Paul Block

New York

For nearly forty years, Kenneth Paul Block was the chief features artist for *Women's Wear Daily* and *W*. A book of his work, *Drawing Fashion: The Art of Kenneth Paul Block*, was published this year.

Franklin Delano Roosevelt was the permanent president during my childhood and youth. There were, of course, political campaigns followed by elections, and through all of that President Roosevelt went right on in his democratically aristocratic way. He was the great leader we needed during a dangerous period, and we knew it.

In his Fireside Chats, broadcast on the radio, we heard the unexpected combination of real concern expressed with elegance. In his effort to find new ways to deal with the frightening disaster of the Great Depression, he introduced and explained, with great clarity, in his splendid diction, new experiments: the NRA, the WPA, the CCC, etcetera. During the 1930s other methods were devised to serve the third of a nation that was ill fed, ill housed, and ill clothed.

His determination to not be seen as crippled was in great part good manners as well as manner. He and Mrs. Roosevelt received the king and queen of England in their Hyde Park house with their usual democratic dignity.

Mrs. Roosevelt's upper-crust style of speech and pronunciation with its loops and swirls in her cultured contralto was much mimicked and satirized; but she, like the president, was devoted to solving economic problems of the oppressed and then later, to facing the grim horrors of war, and trying ultimately for international cooperation.

I am a Democrat because I am waiting for another noble world figure to lead this country. The Republicans do not, will not, and cannot aspire that high.

Of the drawing at right Kenneth says, "It is not a direct illustration of my political affiliation, though she *is* of FDR's era."

Frans de Waal

Georgia

Frans de Waal is a biologist and ethologist whose research focuses on primate social behavior as well as on the origins of morality and justice in human society. He is a professor at Emory University in Atlanta, and is affiliated with the Yerkes National Primate Research Center. His many books include *Primates and Philosophers* and *Our Inner Ape*.

Before Hurricane Katrina struck in 2005, thousands of people with money and cars fled New Orleans, leaving the sick, old, and poor to fend for themselves. It was survival-of-the-fittest writ large. The next morning, my newspaper screamed "Why have we been left behind like animals?" quoting people stuck for days without food and sanitation in the Louisiana Superdome.

I took issue with this headline, not because I felt there was nothing to complain about, but because it irks me that comparisons with animals are made only when people act badly. We love to blame things on biology. In fact, animals don't necessarily leave each other behind. Many animals survive through mutual aid. This applies most definitely to pack hunters, such as wolves or killer whales, but also to our closest relatives, the primates. In Ivory Coast, wild chimpanzees have been seen to care for group mates wounded by leopards, licking their injuries clean, carefully removing dirt, and waving away flies. They protect injured companions and slow down if these can't keep up with their travel. All of this makes perfect sense, given that chimpanzees live in groups for a reason, the same way wolves and humans are group animals for a reason. If man is wolf to man, he is so in every sense, not just the negative one. We would not be where we are today had our ancestors been socially aloof.

The U.S. is a nation with an incredible mismatch between its wealth and its care for its citizens. Katrina offered the most striking example, but it applies to all areas. At the core of any society is the common good. I believe that government needs to guarantee schools of exactly the same quality for rich and poor, and equal access to health care to all people. Clearly, I'd vote Democratic if I were an American citizen.

I come from the Netherlands, where flood protection is taken so seriously that it is kept out of the hands of politicians: it falls under a separate branch of government. There are many things I have come to like about American society, though, not the least of which are its people, otherwise I wouldn't have stayed for over twenty-five years. But its ambivalence toward public services still baffles me. "You get what you pay for," is an American expression, but many people seem to forget this when it comes to taxes and the government.

What we need is a complete overhaul of assumptions about human nature. Biology has been abused long enough to support the goals of a small greedy elite. Obviously, competition is part of human nature, but humans can't live by competition alone. We are hardwired to connect. We flinch at seeing the pain of others, a reaction recently demonstrated in—of all animals—rodents. Empathic responses are as ancient as the mammalian brain.

The idea that Darwinism supports a callous free-market system was introduced, not by Charles Darwin himself, but by a contem-

porary political philosopher. It is obvious that these ideas have
nothing to do with how nature actually operates. There even exists support for a sense of fairness in animals. Experiments with
unequal reward division have shown that one monkey will throw
away a perfectly fine reward, that she normally relishes, if she sees
her companion get an even better one. We are apparently not the
only ones to judge certain social situations unacceptable.

Being an optimist, I do believe this country is ready for a political turnaround that may bring its political system more in line
with what we know about human nature. Even though I cannot
vote, I support the Democrats from the sidelines to build a more
just society and to overcome the fear mongering and unproductive
hatreds of the past eight years.

Who knows? If they succeed, becoming American may regain
its attraction.

Anna Bank

Washington, D.C.

Anna Bank is a member of the Class of 2009
at Georgetown University.

It's unlikely that I'll ever experience three more awkward days
than my freshman orientation at Georgetown two years ago. I can't
even count the number of dining hall conversations that petered
out into silence, with everyone looking around for someone cooler
and more interesting to talk to. At one point, a new acquaintance
had just started to launch into a Bush-bashing quip—you know,
"There's a village in Texas missing its idiot," or something like
that—when she interrupted herself mid-sentence. "Wait," she
said. "You're a Democrat, right?" I assured her that, yes, I was, and
she continued with her story.

On campus, political affiliations are pretty transparent. As an
upper-middle-class Jewish girl from a notoriously liberal college
town, it's obvious which side of the political spectrum I lean toward. I'm a Democrat because I spent the first half of my childhood
in D.C., where the Democratic mayoral primary matters more
than the general election does, and the second half in Madison,
Wisconsin, where there's no such thing as *too* politically correct.
I'm a Democrat because of countless Saturday mornings spent listening to my grandmother scream "Fascists!" at the TV as CNN's

talk-show hosts rehash the latest drama starring Bush, Rove, Cheney, and, back in the day, Bob Dole and Pat Buchanan.

But I'm also a Democrat because I've discovered plenty of reasons to vote blue firsthand. Thirteen years of public school convinced me that American public education has a long way to go, and I know that better-funded schools will get us there much faster than more standardized testing. Sure, I got into Georgetown, but kids whose parents don't have PhDs and MBAs deserve to pass calculus, too. As an aspiring doctor, I think that health care is a right, not a privilege, and it terrifies me to know that millions of Americans are living without health insurance. By the time I get my MD, I want to see some kind of single-payer health care in the works. Hopefully, our next president will make that a reality. And as stereotypical as it is for a college-age woman to fall back on this one, I'm a Democrat because I'm pro-choice. Nothing irks me more than those people holding dead-baby posters on M Street, or the campus pro-life group setting up thousands of tiny pink and blue flags on the front lawn to commemorate aborted fetuses. It's my body and my choice, and I want my government to recognize that.

Even though I'm a dedicated Democrat, I'll be the first to admit that I'm not the most active one in my age bracket by any stretch of the imagination. I haven't interned in Harry Reid's office. I don't recognize members of Congress on the Metro. I'm not even a member of the "Students for Barack Obama" or "One Million Strong for Hillary" Facebook groups, because I haven't chosen a candidate. I won't speak for all college students, but aside from the hardcore—board members of College Dems or College Republicans—it seems like politics is something that most of us fit in somewhere in between problem sets and parties, exercise and extracurriculars, and everything else. But when the election rolls around, I'll definitely be ready to do my democratic (and Democratic) duty.

Acknowledgments

My thanks to PoliPointPress for the opportunity to make this book happen, in particular, editorial director Peter Richardson and publisher Scott Jordan. Thanks as well to PoliPoint's Melissa Edeburn. I am also grateful to David Brock for his eloquent foreword.

Putting together a list of fifty or so typical Democrats was an edifying, entertaining, and, at times, complicated process. The fact is, there is no such thing as "typical" when talking about a party that embraces diversity in the way the Democrats do. For suggesting participants or providing other assistance, my gratitude goes to Jerry Adler, Jim Albrecht, Joan Anderman, Dan Bennett, Ted Bishop, Eric Burns, David Buskin, Sean Cassidy, Joe Conason, Tula Connell, Jane Creech, Chris Darling, Anne Dennin, Steve Dennin, Margot Dougherty, Craig Erkelens, Trevor Fairbrother, Vincent Fitzpatrick of the Enoch Pratt Free Library's Mencken Collection, Beau Friedlander, Jill Gage of the Newberry Library, Bill Glanz, Steven Gragert of the Will Rogers Memorial Museum, Al Habegger, Bea Hartman, Steve Heller, Ellis Henican, Kelly Holder, John Hoyt, Ruth Hunter, Richard Johnson, Sharon Kelly of the JFK Presidential Library, Nicky Lindeman, Sheila McKenna, Matthew Mulcahy, Patricia Mulcahy, Marcel Pariseau, David Peattie, Jan Petrow, Paige Powell, Eric Schmeltzer, Ann Senechal, Katherine Silver, Stephen Silverman, Jim Smith, Michelle Stoneburn, Susan Tarbe, Mandy Vlasz, Sylvia Weiner, and intern James Dennin.

Finally, I offer my sincere thanks to the fifty-five people who contributed their time and their stories to this book. Discussing politics is never simple. Though many participants are and always have been vocal about party affiliation, others have mostly kept quiet about their political leanings. Either way, the nature of this project, and the current state of American politics, led them all to speak openly. Their insights and observations made me proud to belong to the same party.

PoliPointPress will donate a portion of the proceeds from this book to Operation Assist, which provides medical assistance to children and families in the area impacted by Hurricane Katrina. Operation Assist is a collaboration between the Children's Health Fund and the National Center for Disaster Preparedness (NCDP) at the Mailman School of Public Health at Columbia University.

About the Editor

Susan Mulcahy is a writer, editor, and media consultant based in Brooklyn, New York. Her work has appeared in *Vanity Fair*, the *New York Times, O at Home*, and elsewhere. She was formerly editor of the *New York Post*'s Page Six, editor in chief of *Avenue* magazine, and a vice president of Starwave, the early Web content company. She is the producer of CD recordings of monologue artist Ruth Draper and is the author of *My Lips Are Sealed: Confessions of a Gossip Columnist* and *Drawing Fashion: The Art of Kenneth Paul Block*.

Other Books from PoliPointPress

The Blue Pages: A Directory of Companies Rated by Their Politics and Practices

Helps consumers match their buying decisions with their political values by listing the political contributions and business practices of over 1,000 companies. $9.95, paperback.

Jeff Cohen, *Cable News Confidential: My Misadventures in Corporate Media*

Offers a fast-paced romp through the three major cable news channels—Fox CNN, and MSNBC—and delivers a serious message about their failure to cover the most urgent issues of the day. $14.95, paperback.

Marjorie Cohn, *Cowboy Republic: Six Ways the Bush Gang Has Defied the Law*

Shows how the executive branch under President Bush has systematically defied the law instead of enforcing it. $14.95, paperback.

Joe Conason, *The Raw Deal: How the Bush Republicans Plan to Destroy Social Security and the Legacy of the New Deal*

Reveals the well-financed and determined effort to undo the Social Security Act and other New Deal programs. $11.00, paperback.

Kevin Danaher, Shannon Biggs, and Jason Mark, *Building the Green Economy: Success Stories from the Grassroots*

Shows how community groups, families, and individual citizens have protected their food and water, cleaned up their neighborhoods, and strengthened their local economies. $16.00, paperback.

Reese Erlich, *The Iran Agenda: The Real Story of U.S. Policy and the Middle East Crisis*

Explores the turbulent recent history between the two countries and how it has led to a showdown over nuclear technology. $14.95, paperback.

Steven Hill, *10 Steps to Repair American Democracy*

Identifies the key problems with American democracy, especially election practices, and proposes ten specific reforms to reinvigorate it. $11.00, paperback.

Markos Kounalakis and Peter Laufer, *Hope Is a Tattered Flag: Voices of Reason and Change for the Post-Bush Era*

Gathers together the most listened-to politicos and pundits, activists and thinkers, to answer the question: what happens after Bush leaves office? $29.95, hardcover; $16.95 paperback.

Yvonne Latty, *In Conflict: Iraq War Veterans Speak Out on Duty, Loss, and the Fight to Stay Alive*

Features the unheard voices, extraordinary experiences, and personal photographs of a broad mix of Iraq War veterans, including Congressman Patrick Murphy, Tammy Duckworth, Kelly Daugherty, and Camilo Mejia. $24.00, hardcover.

Phillip Longman, *Best Care Anywhere: Why VA Health Care Is Better Than Yours*

Shows how the turnaround at the long-maligned VA hospitals provides a blueprint for salvaging America's expensive but troubled health care system. $14.95, paperback.

Christine Pelosi, *Campaign Boot Camp: Basic Training for Future Leaders*

Offers a seven-step guide for successful campaigns and causes at all levels of government. $15.95, paperback.

William Rivers Pitt, *House of Ill Repute: Reflections on War, Lies, and America's Ravaged Reputation*

Skewers the Bush Administration for its reckless invasions, warrantless wiretaps, lethally incompetent response to Hurricane Katrina, and other scandals and blunders. $16.00, paperback.

Sarah Posner, *God's Profits: Faith, Fraud, and the Republican Crusade for Values Voters*

Examines corrupt televangelists' ties to the Republican Party and unprecedented access to the Bush White House. $19.95, hardcover.

Nomi Prins, *Jacked: How "Conservatives" Are Picking Your Pocket –Whether You Voted For Them or Not*

Describes how the "conservative" agenda has affected your wallet, skewed national priorities, and diminished America—but not the American spirit. $12.00, paperback.

Norman Solomon, *Made Love, Got War: Close Encounters with America's Warfare State*

Traces five decades of American militarism and the media's all-too-frequent failure to challenge it. $24.95, hardcover.

John Sperling et al., *The Great Divide: Retro vs. Metro America*

Explains how and why our nation is so bitterly divided into what the authors call Retro and Metro America. $19.95, paperback.

Daniel Weintraub, *Party of One: Arnold Schwarzenegger and the Rise of the Independent Voter*

Explains how Schwarzenegger found favor with independent voters, whose support has been critical to his success, and suggests that his bipartisan approach represents the future of American politics. $19.95 hardcover.

Curtis White, *The Spirit of Disobedience: Resisting the Charms of Fake Politics, Mindless Consumption, and the Culture of Total Work*

Debunks the notion that liberalism has no need for spirituality and describes a "middle way" through our red state/blue state political impasse. Includes three powerful interviews with John DeGraaf, James Howard Kunstler, and Michael Ableman. $24.00, hardcover.

For more information, please visit www.p3books.com.

About This Book

This book is printed on Cascade Enviro100 Print paper. It contains 100 percent post-consumer fiber and is certified EcoLogo, Processed Chlorine Free, and FSC Recycled. For each ton used instead of virgin paper, we:

- Save the equivalent of 17 trees
- Reduce air emissions by 2,098 pounds
- Reduce solid waste by 1,081 pounds
- Reduce the water used by 10,196 gallons
- Reduce suspended particles in the water by 6.9 pounds.

This paper is manufactured using biogas energy, reducing natural gas consumption by 2,748 cubic feet per ton of paper produced.

The book's printer, Malloy Incorporated, works with paper mills that are environmentally responsible, that do not source fiber from endangered forests, and that are third-party certified. Malloy prints with soy and vegetable based inks, and over 98 percent of the solid material they discard is recycled. Their water emissions are entirely safe for disposal into their municipal sanitary sewer system, and they work with the Michigan Department of Environmental Quality to ensure that their air emissions meet all environmental standards.

The Michigan Department of Environmental Quality has recognized Malloy as a Great Printer for their compliance with environmental regulations, written environmental policy, pollution prevention efforts, and pledge to share best practices with other printers. Their county Department of Planning and Environment has designated them a Waste Knot Partner for their waste prevention and recycling programs.